STIRLING DISTRICT LIBRARIES
3048 00190 7505
D1611974
...ed on or before
...ed below.
ST
Co
11/1/93

EDWIN MUIR

SCOTT AND SCOTLAND

The Predicament of the Scottish Writer

with an introduction by
ALLAN MASSIE

STIRLING
DISTRICT
LIBRARY

POLYGON BOOKS

Published by Polygon Books 1982
1 Buccleuch Place, Edinburgh, EH8 9LW.

First published in Great Britain by
George Routledge & Sons Ltd. 1936.

Copyright © Gavin Muir 1982.
Introduction copyright © Allan Massie 1982.

ISBN 0 904919 60 9

The publisher acknowledges subsidy from the
Scottish Arts Council towards the
publication of this volume.

Cover illustration and design by Charlie Miller.

Typesetting/Layout by E.U.S.P.B.

Reproduced from copy supplied, printed and bound
in Great Britain by Billings & Son Ltd.,
London, Oxford, Worcester.

820.4
MUI

00190 7505

CONTENTS

INTRODUCTION

Literary criticism is generally more ephemeral than fiction, for, by the nature of things, it is usually superseded by new work, while novels gather only the dust of time. The occasional critical work that does, however, survive, is as often as much a piece of propaganda as of criticism. In such books the writer has a point of view which may be only tangential to whatever he purports to criticize; their value lies in the general argument rather than in any detailed examination of a text, and that argument will probably be related to the author's immediate concern, a concern, that is, that operates on creative work he seeks to do himself. The criticism of Dryden, Johnson, Coleridge, Eliot, Pound and James belongs to this category; the greatest and most enduringly fresh critics tend to be practitioners of the art they criticize. Edwin Muir's *Scott and Scotland* is an example of such a book. For all its slightness, it is a book which has been more influential than any other single piece of Scottish literary criticism; a book, deeply resented and fiercely attacked, yet one which still reads freshly today.

It was meant, as Muir tells us in the first paragraph, to be one of a series in which, according to "the original intention . . . a writer should select some figure or subject and inquire what he or it had done for Scotland". Muir was allotted Sir Walter Scott, but, scarcely had he started than he saw that "a much more promising subject for inquiry would be what Scotland had done for him. This very quickly led me to consider the question of the writer in Scotland generally, a position which is both unhappy and unique." Hence he was led to ask whether there was actually such a thing as Scottish literature and, if so, "in what sense it could be called a literature".

Scott thus became a peg on which Muir could hang a general argument, the fount of which remained however his perception of what he felt to be "a very curious emptiness behind the wealth of Scott's imagination". Scott criticism has advanced since Muir's day — he was writing, after all, only a few years after E. M. Forster had contrived to discover that Scott had "a trivial mind and a heavy style . . . neither artistic detachment nor passion" — and few would now be quite so certain of this emptiness; but, for Muir's purpose, it was essential that it should be there so that he could account for "this hiatus in his endowment . . . by invoking the fact — if" (he adds charmingly) "the reader will allow that it is one — that he lived most of his days in a hiatus, in a country, that is to say, which was neither a nation nor a province, but had, instead of a centre, a blank, an Edinburgh, in the middle of it".

This is a very curious thing to say, for two reasons. First, Muir omits the one thing that Scotland certainly wasn't — that is to say, a State — and prefers to substitute the dubious assertion that it wasn't a nation. Since Muir, with his extensive knowledge of Central Europe, must have known that nations could survive without Statehood, one finds oneself asking why he makes this substitution; and it is not till the last pages of the book, when he rejects the Scottish nationalist solution for Scotland's ills, that the answer becomes clear. For it is then evident that, if the restoration of Statehood could repair "the broken kingdom", then much of Muir's general argument would dissolve. It is essential for his purposes to stress that Scotland's ills go deeper than, and precede, the effects of the Union.

Secondly, something of the same sort explains the rest of this remarkable sentence: "instead of a centre, a blank, an Edinburgh, in the middle of it". This might well be a fair description of Muir's Scotland, but it hardly seems adequate as a representation of Scott's, when this blank, this Edinburgh, was still the city of Enlightenment, home of the most intellectually stimulating university in the United Kingdom, and of the foremost reviews of the day. To admit this, however, would have gone against the grain of his argument; so, with that beautiful lucidity of his, which leapt awkward facts with the ease of a Romantic Highlander skipping over the heather, he erases the real Edinburgh that Scott lived in, and substitutes, with an audacity one can only admire, "a blank".

Such recklessness reveals *Scott and Scotland* to be a work of polemics. Scott himself becomes a broadsword to be used in the Civil War of the self-styled Scottish Renaissance. The argument was about language, the point to be resolved how a Scottish writer in his "unhappy and unique" position should write. If Muir could show how a man of Scott's genius (which he admits) had been dished, "so that he left his picture of life in such a tentative state", then he might be able to decide by what means a Scottish writer might come to completeness".

"There is at present," he adds, "a general disposition in Scotland to blame Scottish writers who turn to the English tradition . . . I shall have to consider whether they should do so, or rather whether they have any choice but to do so." Otherwise, the Scottish writer "will find neither an organic community to round off his conceptions, nor a major literary tradition to support him, nor even a faith among the people themselves that a Scottish literature is possible or desirable, nor any opportunity, finally, of making a livelihood by his work". The problem of literature in Scotland "cannot be solved by writing poems in Scots, or by looking forward to some hypothetical Scotland in the future".

This then is what Muir intends to demonstrate; to this extent the work is an anti-MacDiarmid. If, however, it was merely that, it would be only of local, and now historical, interest. It is certain, however, that the problems Muir identifies are still before us today; the arguments of the relation of a writer to language and culture are still interesting; the predicament of the Scottish writer is hardly happier than it was then. Eric Linklater agreed with Muir that the lack of vitality in the Scottish novel was an index of disbelief in Scottish society, and wrote: "novelists may avoid Scottish themes; or deal with them in a parochial spirit that belittles what is already small enough; or confine themselves to some remote parcel of geography, to some distant fragment of life and find in that solitary corner a significance that is clearly lacking in the whole". This argument chimes with Muir's; it still confronts us. It is the endurance of the dilemma, as much as the manner of writing and the cogency of much of the argument, which keeps *Scott and Scotland* fresh and relevant.

* * *

It might seem strange that in a book ostensibly about Scott Muir should spend so much time discussing poetry; for, though Scott was undeniably a poet, and a fine one, his novels are obviously his greatest work. Yet Muir's angle of approach was, given his purposes, wisely chosen, and justifiable, for it is in poetry that the use of language may be most effectively studied, and the argument Muir was engaged in was essentially about language.

He wished to show that Scotland had once indeed had a literature, but had lost it for a variety of reasons. The consequence of this loss was that Scotsmen existed in a state of linguistic uncertainty, so that, in his most celebrated phrase, we "feel in one language and think in another". Since "the prerequisites of an autonomous literature is a homogeneous language", our culture was broken. "Every genuine literature," he says, "requires as its condition a means of expression capable of dealing with everything the mind can think or the imagination can conceive. It must be a language for criticism as well as poetry, for abstract speculation as well as fact, and, since we live in a scientific age, it must be a language for science as well." Any language which could serve only some of these purposes must be considered "an anachronism . . . as a vehicle for literature". For he contended (surely rightly) "in an organic literature poetry is always influencing prose, and prose poetry; and their interaction energizes them both".

Muir's style is a Pope's; he writes with the cool authority of an Encyclical. It is also courteous, and the combination is likely to disarm the uncommitted reader. When he goes on to demonstrate that Scots was once such "a homogeneous literary language", but is so no longer, so that we are now placed in a situation in which "the mind is divorced from the feelings so decisively that each uses a language of its own" with the result that "the one can exercise only a very imperfect influence on the other"; that, consequently, a poet writing in Scots cannot even criticize his own work, since the language of criticism is different from the language of composition; and when he supports this theory by a diversity of well-chosen quotations which do indeed seem to indicate that this divorce of feeling and thought has taken place; well then, one is tempted to throw up one's hands, and concede the game.

Nevertheless there are still some points to be made on the other side, points which are not merely exercises in debating skill, but which may enrich, while complicating, the argument. Muir's very cogent lucidity does lead him to simplify things excessively, to omit what is jagged or disruptive to his argument. It encourages him to use terms which he never properly defines, but which have a pleasing ring (just what exactly, for instance, is "an organic community" when the term is used for something bigger than an Orkney parish, and how would we recognize one?). Finally, this lucidity may lead him to distort his argument, for lucidity is often the result of a narrow vision, and Muir's argument gains point, but loses authority, by being confined narrowly to Scotland.

First though, certain of his contentions should be admitted. It is true that Scotland in the fifteenth and sixteenth centuries produced poetry displaying a union of thought and feeling, which had hardly been achieved since; and that this is evidence that pre-Reformation Scotland possessed "a high culture of the feelings as well as of the mind". It is true that this poetry did not develop, as might have been expected, in such a way as to foster a poetic drama. It is true that what Muir, pejoratively but justly, calls dialect poetry has produced nothing to equal this; and it is true, as his comparison of Dunbar and Burns very justly shows, that the Renaissance poet was writing "in a self-subsistent language" and the dialect one "in a sort of ragtag of phrases, neither ordinary speech nor poetic diction"; and that this difference testifies to the earlier poet's fortune in having a language capable of dealing with what he both thought and felt. In short, Muir's examination of the poetry he produces as evidence seems to me exemplary and almost irrefutable.

What, however, of his conclusions? What took the place of this high culture, he says, "was either simple irresponsible feeling side by side with arid intellect, or else that reciprocally destructive confrontation of both for which Gregory Smith found the name of 'the

Caledonian Antisyzygy': a recognition that they are irreconcilable, and that Scottish life is split in two without remedy". What of this? And what of the assertion that this split is made manifest in our linguistic confusion?

Well, these conclusions follow logically on the argument if all the premises are sound. But are they? Some of the planks on which Muir rests his thesis have a wormy look to me.

First, though we agree to call the language of the Makars Scots, Dunbar himself called it English. For him Scots was Gaelic, and though undoubtedly there are differences between the language of James IV's Court and the language of Henry VII's, these differences are not great. Often they seem little more than matters of orthography, presumably representing different accent and pronunciation. When Muir gives us beautiful passages from Henryson's *Testament of Cresseid*, or Mark Alexander Boyd's sonnet "Fra bank to bank, fra wood to wood I rin", or Alexander Scott's "Lo, what it is to luve", or the anonymous poem from the Bannantyne MS that begins "My heart is heigh above/my body is full of bliss", I would agree that this is poetry such as has not been written in Scotland since; but I also find hardly a word or a piece of syntax that would have puzzled a contemporary Englishman. This is surprising — Dunbar after all regarded Chaucer as his master: "O reuerend Chaucer, rose of rethoris all/As in oure tong ane flour imperiall, that raise in Britane evir, who redis rycht,/Thou bearis of makaris the tryumph riall". (In the same poem, he says of the Englishmen Gower and Lydgate that "Your angel mouthis most mellifluate/Our rude language has clere illumynate".) It might seem strange that Muir should have ignored this, for, after all, the thrust of his argument is that Scottish writers should employ English; and this would seem to be supported by the practice and opinions of the Makars themselves. But to make such an admission would be to remove the plank that supports his assertion that Scots think in one language and feel in another, and leave the judgement dangling in mid-air; for that argument depends on maintaining and exaggerating the difference between Scots and English, a difference that MacDiarmid, with his delving in dictionaries for obsolete words, and the practice of bringing together dialect words to create a "synthetic Scots", certainly both emphasized and encouraged.

Second, there is a strange dislocation within Muir's own argument. While on the one hand he maintains that pre-Reformation Scotland possessed the high culture which is only possible when there is a homogeneous language capable of being employed for all purposes, on the other he admits that "Scots is without a prose, that is as a separate vehicle for thought". Though he (defensively?) adds "we cannot doubt if its development had continued it would have had such a prose", we may still legitimately find it odd that Muir should happily postulate the existence of the "highest culture" dependent on there being "a homogeneous" language, if he then admits that one of his own prerequisites for such a culture and such a language is nowhere to be found. And indeed it would be odd if language was quite the straitjacket Muir seems to think it is.

INTRODUCTION

The relationship between literature and language, and writers and language (for the two are not the same thing), is perhaps more complicated than Muir seems to have realized; and much work has, of course, been done on it since his day, particularly in France. I have no space to elaborate the arguments here, but a few points may be briefly made.

First, writers are less imprisoned in a single language than Muir would have us believe. The case of Mediaeval and Renaissance Latin poetry illustrates this. (It might be noted incidentally that the Scots poetic drama which, as Muir observes, failed to develop, was actually written by George Buchanan in Latin; neglected now, because few can read it, and fewer still would understand it in the theatre, it was nevertheless admired and successful in its own day.) Muir might object that one certainly cannot fairly compare the writing of sixteenth-century Latin to the composition of Scots verse, for Latin was an acquired language, not "the language of sentiment imbibed at the mother's knee". Yet, for some poets who have written in Scots (Lallans) since Muir's time, the case has been in this way similar to that of the Renaissance Latinist. Sydney Goodsir Smith is the best example. Born in New Zealand, educated at Malvern and Oxford, he acquired Scots, as a man might set himself to learn to write Latin poetry; his mature work, *Under the Eildon Tree*, is rich Scots and fine poetry.

The ability of a writer to move between languages is something that the thrust of Muir's argument is bound to ignore. Yet it cannot be forgotten. How does the formula "thinking in one language and feeling in another" account for these Latinists? How does it accommodate a Conrad or a Nabokov; those American Jewish writers brought up by Yiddish-speaking Mommas and Grandmothers? a Kipling whose first language was Urdu? those writers who seem to move with happy facility between one language and another, like Iain Crichton Smith between Gaelic and English? Is Walter Scott himself more or less a poet when he interpolates a verse in a Scots ballad or writes an exquisite lyric in English like Proud Maisie or Lucy Ashton's song?

Muir might fairly object. He might say that the case of Scott proves nothing, for he has never denied that dialect Scots can do some jobs; what he does assert is that Scots is not, and has not for long been, an autonomous language which can be used for a complete literature. Yet, even if one grants this, it is hard to see why Scott's possession of dialect Scots should be regarded as more disabling than Hardy's Wessex dialect or George Eliot's Warwickshire. Scott could not write novels or substantial poetry in dialect any more than they could, but his possession of it enriched his work in the same way as their mastery of dialect enriched theirs. The comparison suggests, once again, that the distinction between Scots and English is by no means as absolute or unique as Muir would have us think. And if it isn't, then perhaps the reasons for the sorry state of Scottish culture are less purely linguistic either.

Secondly, Muir might say that a literature is, of course, something different from, and more than, the peculiarities and talents of individual writers. A homogeneous literature provides us with a heritage, and Muir's case was that Scotland lacked this, and that the lack inhibited even Walter Scott. No one can deny the truth of part of this argument, especially if one narrows one's definition of what is Scots and Scottish as Muir does. For Muir, the writer is enclosed in language. He might agree with Barthes that language "enfolds the whole of literary creation much as the earth, the sky, and the line where they meet outline a familiar habitat for mankind". The problem for the Scottish writer was that the horizon of his native country was too low, while if he moved over to English, he found himself abroad and ill-at-ease. For Muir, insistent on the difference between the two languages (an insistence, to be fair, that had been vociferously maintained by his adversaries in the Civil War), the only solution was for the writer to acclimatize himself to that foreign country of the English language "No one," says Barthes again, "can without formalities pretend to insert his freedom as a writer into the resistant medium of language because, behind the latter, the whole of History stands unified and complete in the manner of a Natural Order." Yet this is what MacDiarmid was trying to do; he was denying History, and, if he was doing it with certain formalities, Muir hadn't noticed or didn't care. Certainly there is something absurd about the spectacle of a writer setting himself up against History — there is always something absurd about self-conscious Titanry; and it is equally the case that many poets who have followed MacDiarmid have worn their Scots narcissistically; they have been as ridiculous as the writer who feels he must don a dressing-gown à la Balzac before settling at his desk. Yet it is the case too that Writing also exists as Freedom. The writer can choose, as MacDiarmid chose; and any successful outcome, however partial, itself becomes part of the tradition the next generation inherits.

The word "tradition" brings us back to the other weakness that Muir's narrow concentration on the Scots-or-English contest leads him into, and yet to disguise in his argument. And this error vitiates his view of Scott.

Muir's whole argument depends ultimately on the evidence he presents for the decline in culture since the sixteenth century, and his harnessing of this evidence to the language question, leading to the conclusion that Scots think in one language and feel in another.

"Something," Muir says, was lost to Scottish poetry after the sixteenth century and has never been recovered since, a quality which might be called wholeness." After this time, sentiment is divorced from thought. After this time, Scots poetry offers only the "simple unforced lyric" or "wild irresponsible fantasy governed by intellect". The argument is powerful, but it is only half-true.

Muir sets "my heart is neigh above" against "My luve is like a red, red rose"; and he might say:

"The difference is not a simple difference of degree between poets. It is something which had happened to the mind of Scotland between the time of the anonymous poet of the Bannantyne MS and Burns; it is the difference between the intellectual poet and the reflective one. Burns is a poet and he thinks; but he does not feel his

thought. A thought to the sixteenth-century poet was an experience; it modified his sensibility. . . .
. . . We may express the difference by the following theory: the poets of the sixteenth century possessed a mechanism of sensibility which could devour any experience . . . then a dissociation of sensibility sets in, from which we have never fully recovered. . . ."

This is a fair representation of Muir's argument, and he might have said it. Only, of course, he didn't; because this is not Muir, but Eliot. All I have done is substituted "the anonymous poet" for "Donne", "Burns" for "Tennyson and Browning" and "the sixteenth century" for the "seventeenth". It is perfectly obvious that Muir and Eliot are talking about the same thing; that the dissocation of sensibility cannot be restricted to Scotland; and that Francis Bacon and the scientific revolution have their part to play as well as John Knox and the dwindling of Scots to dialect status.

Muir then exaggerates. While he is scrupulous in insisting that other reasons than the linguistic one contribute to Scotland's "loss of civilization", nevertheless his concentration on languages, a concentration that is perfectly understandable when we consider his immediate polemical purposes, means that he ignores the extent to which what happened to Scotland was a cultural experience characteristic of the age rather than of the nation. The separation of thinking and feeling, inasmuch as one can identify it, is a Western European, not a purely Scottish, phenomenon. If it perhaps took a starker form here — and there is a good case for saying that it did — then reasons other than linguistic should account for this.

For, as we have seen, the gulf between Scots and English was not as wide as both the proponents and adversaries of Lallans would have us believe. It is too simple to say that Scots think in one language and feel in another; the beauty of Muir's antithesis has been too easily accepted. Our cultural heritage is more complex than that. Muir's aphorism, employed to explain Walter Scott, in the end obscures and belittles his achievement. We are talking about variants of a single language, not about distinct tongues.

Yet, this said, what a wealth of thought remains in Muir's argument. The questions he poses remain before us. We still seek something to explain the dearth of literature in Scotland after the Reformation. No matter how we may question Muir's argument in detail, we still cannot find anything satisfactorily to account for the failure to develop, the inability to recover from the dissociation of sensibility as English literature recovered with Dryden, Pope and Johnson; where, we wonder, is the Scottish Wordsworth; or rather, why is there no such being?

We cannot deny what Muir perceived; that Scott had to invent for himself the Scottish elements of a tradition in which it was possible to write fiction. And though Muir may have underestimated the ability of a writer of genius to do this, and so failed to appreciate that what MacDiarmid had done in Scots might make it possible for other writers to do more — not necessarily greater, but different; nevertheless part of the argument stands.

* * *

It is generally agreed that what Muir has to say directly about Scott is less interesting, less remarkable and less provocative (in the best, constructive sense of the word) than what he says about Scottish literature in general. P. H. Scott, in his recent (and admirable) book, *Walter Scott and Scotland*, even goes so far as to say that Muir's book "had very little to do with Scott himself, and I do not have the impression that Muir had read much of Scott or thought much about him".

Such judgements can neither be proved nor disproved. All one can say is that while Muir had thought about Scott sufficiently to employ him very effectively for his immediate purpose, he too easily accepted the view of Scott held in progressive circles at the time he was writing, and that his concentration on the linguistic issue led him into some strangely contradictory statements.

Muir can hardly be blamed for failing to see how Scott would be read today, and he might well be surprised by his present standing. Yet in fairness it should be said that Muir had contributed to this revaluation. The errors of a critic can be as fertile of new readings as his choicer strokes. So A. O. J. Cockshut (*The Achievement of Sir Walter Scott*), seizing on Muir's Scots for feeling, English for thinking formula, and on Virginia Woolf's observation that "the lifeless English gives way to the living Scots", finds on the contrary that "Scott turned to artistic gain the disastrous division of Scots culture and language into rational English and feeling Scots. . . . For him the analytical English paragraphs were the way of coming to understand, assimilate and judge the strong, and sometimes wild emotions expressed by his characters in the vernacular. Unless a novel makes a pattern, it is no more than a set of anecdotes. Meg Merrilees, Baron Bradwardine and the rest, need not only to be felt but to be understood. Scott's dual method ensures that they are."

Far therefore from finding, like Muir, "a curious emptiness behind the wealth of his imagination", the modern critic discovers that Scott is capable of making a fruitful synthesis of his cultural heritage and experience.

Muir's criticism of Scott is a thing of brilliant flashes, shedding no steady light. He rightly sees that Scott "was by instinct a Conservative who believed in the established order and tradition. But the phase Scotland had reached in his time involved him in a divided allegiance. . . . He adhered to the established order of the United Kingdom. . . . But at the same time he saw this established order gradually destroying another established order, that of Scotland. That order was equally old, equally rooted in history and sanctified by the past, and moreover it was the order to which he was most intimately bound by birth, early memory and the compulsion of his imagination. From this inward conflict he never escaped. It is the underlying theme of his three great novels, *Old Mortality, The Heart of Midlothian* and *Redgauntlet*; and it is deeply entangled with all his stories of Scottish life except the more purely contemporary and local ones such as *Guy Mannering*."

This is finely put, and we cannot doubt that Scott's intellect and imagination were exercised by this conflict. But as a statement of what actually happens in these novels it is inadequate; it misrepresents Scott's philosophy of history and his understanding of how History works itself out; while the final qualification displays Muir's own, perhaps barely apprehended, dissatisfaction with his own theory. For, if this "inward conflict" was so inescapable, shouldn't it have been most apparent where Muir confessedly finds it absent, namely in those novels that deal with contemporary Scotland?

Novels cannot be fitted into the confines of such single explanations. Nowhere is this more evident than in Muir's sympathetic treatment of *Redgauntlet*. Muir rightly sees that *Redgauntlet* is a novel "with a splendour of passion, and a sense of great forces overarching and environing the action itself". He observes that "Redgauntlet himself seems to come more wholly out of what Lord Tweedsmuir calls Scott's 'secret world' than any other character he ever created". And he finds that in "the fine interview between Redgauntlet and his nephew Darsie one has the feeling that Scott is uttering his deepest convictions as he rarely did elsewhere".

The interview is extensively quoted in the text so that I shall not reproduce it in this introductory note; but this must be said, that the passage is misleading if read out of its context of the novel. And Muir's criticism of it appears to be based on such a reading. He makes it sound as if Scott himself is to be wholly identified with his creation, as if there is no corrective. But the novel abounds in such correctives, and Scott is no more to be saddled with Redgauntlet's despair, than Edgar's reflection in Lear "as flies to wanton boys are we to the gods/they kill us for their sport" is to be taken as Shakespeare's last word on human life. The novel is something much richer and more complicated than Muir will allow, and Redgauntlet, for all his splendour of utterance, is a character whose understanding of life has been distorted by his addiction to rhetoric and the histrionic posture. Any reading of the novel should make this clear; Redgauntlet has all the attributes of a tragic hero, but he has so, partly because, in pursuit of a political ideal, he has failed to cultivate the warm human qualities. Scott knows this perfectly well. He has let us have Darsie Latimer's naively Romantic picture of the man; he has also given us Alan Fairford's reductive one. Neither is adequate, any more than is Redgauntlet's own view of himself as an embattled Titan. Yet all contain truth; all contribute to the complete picture.

Redgauntlet, the novel, by itself, is enough to explode Muir's notion of the emptiness behind the wealth of Scott's imagination, for the novel is characterized by the rich maturity of its central conception. Furthermore, this great passage, in which Redgauntlet sees the collapse of all his hopes, a passage which Muir himself describes as "the finest in the heroic style that Scott ever wrote", like that other when Redgauntlet responds to his nephew's claim to free will with the words "the true cant of the day" (both passages throbbing with the profoundest feeling), is written in the purest, most classical English; so much, one may say, for Muir's division of feeling and thought.

The fact is that in his consideration of novels, Muir's determination to use Scott as a stick with which to beat MacDiarmid distorts and traduces what it purports to examine. It is only too evident that Scott cannot be confined within the boundaries the critic has drawn. Muir asks why Scott "reached back into the past of history" and came up with the answer that he did so in order "to win a complete theme on which to write and complete order in which to write". "This led him," he continues, "to stuff his head with the most nonsensical trash to use his own words; the trash being trash and nonsensical because it had little reference to the Scotland of his own time, and because the events with which it dealt were already settled for good. . . ." The quotation is of course a misquotation. As P. H. Scott has pointed out, a reading of the Ashestiel Memoir makes it quite clear that the trash referred to was his vast reading in chivalric romances, nothing to do with the Scotland of the great novels at all. In the same way Muir sees the writing of *The Lay of the Last Minstrel* as an attempt of the same sort, "in a present that was melting and dissolving away". But Scott himself accounted for it otherwise; he had written it, he told Wordsworth, "to discharge my mind of the ideas which from infancy have rushed upon it". He "thus expelled the Fiend of chivalry".

Scott set his fiction in the past because his whole cast of mind was historical; he was a product of that Edinburgh of the Enlightenment which had been dominated by the philosophical historians. "I believe this is the historical age and this the historical nation," wrote David Hume. "History for them," writes P. H. Scott, "was not a disjointed and haphazard series of events, but could be shown to have a pattern and significance." The Waverley novels dramatize the historical process. Far from being escapist, Scott's decision to set his novels in the past reveals his understanding that only this sort of novel could properly account for the present.

* * *

It may seem that I am concerned to belittle Muir; some may ask why I should choose to write an introduction to a book with which I so evidently quarrel. Both objections may be answered briefly. On the one hand, the merits of a work are often to be found in the questions it raises rather than the answers it gives; on the other Muir's analysis of the predicament of the Scottish writer is hardly invalidated by some misreadings and some over-simplifications. *Scott and Scotland* remains a work of the first importance, not because one has to agree with everything Muir says, not because one has even to accept the general line of his argument, but because it is a book which makes one think. Nobody concerned with the condition of Scottish culture can ignore it; nobody so concerned can fail to profit from perusing it.

In one respect, the controversy in which Muir engaged himself, is stilled. Nobody, I take it, will now fight a duel for or against Lallans. A Scottish writer will now use it or not use it as it seems useful. We can recognize that we have at our disposal a whole range of language, from unaccented Received Standard English to the most clotted, or would-be aureate, synthetic Scots, or the demotic Glaswegian employed by writers like Tom Leonard. And though one may recognize the truth of Muir's observation that the further a writer moves from English, the harder it is to apply any useful criticism to his work, nevertheless we have a sufficient body of work in varieties of Scots for some sort of critical standard to be possible; though it must be admitted that it will be rather academic criticism, as for instance a Latinist can distinguish between good and bad Virgil.

Yet in other respects our condition has worsened since Muir wrote, and our predicament is certainly graver than Scott's was. For in his day, even if Scotland was no longer a State, and even if its national peculiarities were being blurred, Scotland remained what very evidently Muir, an acute but unhistorical critic, couldn't see that it was, distinct to itself. Now, we cannot be certain of that. Scott's Scotland retained a public life; ours has none; or at least it has none that can invigorate, or prove fertile, to a writer. The writer thus lives in a society which has abandoned responsibility for its own direction, and which, by allowing its "peculiar features" to be smoothed away, finds that whole sectors of it do no more than reflect a way of life that is lived more intensely and urgently elsewhere. Accordingly, Scottish novelists achieve their surest success when they treat of life on the geographical periphery where manners do remain distinct, or in that one area, our decaying industrial heartland, where, for sombre historical reasons, we do actually experience more intensely and more colourfully, afflictions common to other formerly dynamic cultures now left behind by progress. Clydeside by this reading is this century's Jacobite theme; the problem for the writer is to place it as Scott placed Redgauntlet.

The tragedy of Scottish literature and civilization is that no writer of genius succeeded Scott, able to do for the nineteenth century what he had done for the seventeenth and eighteenth. The wrong lessons were learned from his work; people attached themselves to one strand in his tapestry and reworked it colourfully. The one man of genius in the generation that succeeded his — Carlyle — found that Scottish intellectual society offered him insufficient nourishment and departed to London, but it would be as true to say that Carlyle failed Scotland as to put it the other way round. Indeed, there is some absurdity inherent in the notion that a country can fail a writer, for a country, conceived in this sense, is no more than a metaphysical idea. Muir reversed the question he was originally set to answer, partly because his misreading, as it seems to me, of Scott enabled him to say that Scotland "could not give him a basis for the profound criticism of life of which there is no doubt that he was capable . . .". If, however, we find in Scott just such a profound criticism, then much of Muir's argument inevitably falls away, and the original question regains its point. What did Scott do for Scotland?

And the answer seems clear. He gave Scotland consciousness of its own history and nature. By doing so, he supplied what had certainly, as Muir points out, been lacking: a cultural heritage. He contrived beyond what might have been thought possible, to assimilate English and European influences, and to create out of this something distinctively and unmistakeably Scottish and modern; his method was seized on and developed elsewhere. But not in Scotland; here Scott's heirs tended to imitate what was most imitable but least important. The result is that we are still waiting for the writer who can usefully learn from Scott. And this is not surprising. Genius casts a long shadow. Shakespeare destroyed Blank Verse as a medium for drama. Milton as one for Epic. Such writers occupy territory and hold it against all-comers. So far, then, Scott has done more for readers than for writers; he continues to supply us with a good part of our understanding of what it means to be Scottish.

In one sense the predicament of the Scottish writer is brought about by non-literary causes. It is how to treat of a country that has become a sham; it is how to work in an intensely philistine nation. These problems have appeared since Scott's time. In another more narrowly literary sense, it is how to come to terms with Walter Scott, and how to make use of what he made. Muir's book, despite its frequent wrong-headedness, is still not only intensely interesting, but immediately valuable in this task.

ALLAN MASSIE

ACKNOWLEDGMENTS

I wish to express my thanks and acknowledgments to Lord Tweedsmuir and Messrs. Cassell and Company for permission to quote at length from *Sir Walter Scott*, by John Buchan; to Messrs. Macmillan and Company for certain passages taken from G. Gregory Smith's *Scottish Literature: Character and Influence*; and to Messrs. J. M. Dent and Sons for extracts from Miss M. M. Gray's anthology, *Scottish Poetry from Barbour to James VI.* I have used Miss Gray's admirable modernisation of the old spelling, as I considered this most suitable for a book such as the present one, which is a general survey of the state of Scottish Literature, and makes no pretence to exact scholarship.

E.M.

INTRODUCTORY

The original intention of this series was that a number of writers should select some figure or subject and inquire what he or it had done for Scotland. The figure allotted to me was Walter Scott. I began to discover what he had done for Scotland, but had scarcely started before I saw that a much more promising subject for inquiry would be what Scotland had done for him. This very quickly led me to consider the position of the writer in Scotland generally, a position which is both unhappy and unique. That in turn raised the whole question of Scottish literature, of which so much has been written during the last decade; and I felt driven to ask whether Scotland could be said to have a literature, and if so, in what sense it could be called a literature. Here the only standards I could appeal to were comparative. I knew three literatures passably well — the English, the French, and the German. They had the advantage of being fairly familiar to most educated people, so that the comparison could generally be between a thing known and a thing known, which is indispensable for useful comparison. All three literatures (but the first and second in particular) were also sufficiently rich and complete to serve as standards for what an autonomous literature should be. But I found I could not consider literature without considering language too, for language is the vehicle of literature; and so I had finally to come back to the Scottish language which is the most controversial aspect of my subject.

A separate volume could easily be written on each of these questions. My justification for treating them so briefly is necessity. I could not deal with the problem of what Scotland did for Scott, and following on that, what Scotland has done and is still doing for the writer, without taking them all into account, as well indeed as several more which will arise in the course of my argument. The riddle which confronted me in approaching Scott himself, by far the greatest creative force in Scottish literature as well as one of the greatest in English, was to account for a very curious emptiness which I felt behind the wealth of his imagination. Many critics have acknowledged this blemish in Scott's work, but have either made no attempt to account for it, or else have put it down to a defect in Scott's mind and character. Yet men of Scott's enormous genius have rarely Scott's faults; they may have others but not these particular ones; and so I was forced to account for the hiatus in Scott's endowment by considering the environment in which he lived, by invoking the fact — if the reader will agree it is one — that he spent most of his days in a hiatus, in a country, that is to say, which was neither a nation nor a province, and had, instead of a centre, a blank, an Edinburgh, in the middle of it. But this Nothing in which Scott wrote was not merely a spatial one; it was a temporal Nothing as well, dotted with a few disconnected figures arranged at abrupt intervals: Henryson, Dunbar, Allan Ramsay, Burns, with a rude buttress of ballads and folk songs to shore them up and keep them from falling. Scott, in other words, lived in a community which was not a community, and set himself to carry on a tradition which was not a tradition; and the result was that his work was an exact reflection of his predicament. His picture of life had no centre, because the environment in which he lived had no centre. What traditional virtue his work possessed was at second hand, and derived mainly from English literature, which he knew intimately but which was a semi-foreign literature to him. Scotland did not have enough life of its own to nourish a writer of his scope; it had neither a real community to foster him nor a tradition to direct him; for the anonymous ballad tradition was not sufficient for his genius. So that my inquiry into what Scotland did for Scott came down finally to what it did not do for Scott. What it did not do, or what it could not do. Considered historically these alternatives are difficult to separate.

Having traced Scott's greatest fault to his geographical and historical position as a writer, I began to wonder what he might have been, given his genius, if he had been born into a genuine organic society such as England, or even into a small self-subsistent state like Weimar. Could he possibly have left his picture of life in such a tentative state, half flesh and blood and half pasteboard, unreal where he dealt with highly civilized people, and real where he dealt with peasants, adventurers and beggars? Would he not have been forced to give it unity? or rather, would not a sociological unity at least have been there without his having to make a specific effort to achieve it? To ask such questions is not criticism; but the object of this book is not criticism. I wish merely to define the position of the Scottish writer, and then to inquire by what means he can come to completeness, what help Scotland can give him in doing so, and what obstacles she puts in his way. There is at present a general disposition in Scotland to blame Scottish writers who turn to the English tradition when they are faced with this problem. I shall have to consider whether they should do so, or rather whether they have any choice but to do so.

But behind this problem of the Scottish writer there is another which, if not for the individual author, for Scotland itself is of crucial importance. This is the problem of Scottish literature, and it is clearly a question for the Scottish people as a whole, not for the individual Scottish writer; for only a people can create a literature. The practical present-day problem may be put somewhat as follows: that a Scottish writer who wishes to achieve some approximation to completeness has no choice except to absorb the English tradition, and that if he thoroughly does so his work belongs not merely to Scottish literature but to English literature as well. On the other hand, if he wishes to add to an indigenous Scottish literature, and roots himself deliberately in Scotland, he will find there, no matter how long he may search, neither an organic community to round off his conceptions, nor a major literary tradition to support him, nor even a faith among the people themselves that a Scottish literature is possible or desirable, nor any opportunity, finally, of making a livelihood by his work. All these things are part of a single problem which can only be understood by considering Scottish literature historically, and the qualities in the Scottish people which have made them what they are; it cannot be solved by writing poems in Scots, or by looking forward to some hypothetical Scotland in the future.

That is the problem, in the most simple terms I can find for it; and it appears to me that Scots criticism has largely ignored it.

I

SCOTTISH LITERATURE

1. LANGUAGE

Scottish literature, considered linguistically, may be divided into Early Scots, Middle Scots, and Anything At All. The first two periods exhibit a certain homogeneity of language and as a result of that a definite style; the third, which began tentatively with Knox (the first Scotsman to write good English prose), and definitely with the acceptance of the English translation of the Bible, signalizes a disintegration of the language of Scottish literature and the disappearance of a distinctive Scottish style. Scotland continued to produce writers, but they wrote in a confusion of tongues ranging from orthodox English to the dialects of the various Scottish districts. The only speech which they did not continue to use was Scots, for that had disappeared. Consequently, since some time in the sixteenth century Scottish literature has been a literature without a language. Middle Scots survived Sir David Lyndsay for a while in the lyrics of Alexander Scott and Montgomery. But a little later Drummond of Hawthornden was already writing in pure English, and since then Scottish poetry has been written either in English, or in some local dialect, or in some form of synthetic Scots, such as Burns's, or Scott's, or Hugh MacDiarmid's. Scottish prose disappeared altogether, swept away by Knox's brilliant *History of the Reformation* and the Authorized Version of the Bible.

The reasons for this disintegration of the language of Scottish literature are controversial, and I have no space to enter into them here. But it is clear that the Reformation, the Union of the Crowns, and the Union of the Kingdoms had all a great deal to do with it. I must confine myself, however, to certain of its consequences. The prerequisite of an autonomous literature is a homogeneous language. If Shakespeare had written in the dialect of Warwickshire, Spenser in Cockney, Ralegh in the broad Western English speech which he used, the future of English literature must have been very different, for it would have lacked a common language where all the thoughts and feelings of the English people could come together, add lustre to one another, and serve as a standard for one another. A common language of this kind can only be conceived, it seems to me, as an achievement continuously created and preserved by the highest spiritual energy of a people: the nursing ground and guarantee of all that is best in its thought and imagination: and without it no people can have any standard of literature. For this homogeneous language is the only means yet discovered for expressing the response of a whole people, emotional and intellectual, to a specific body of experience peculiar to it alone, on all levels of thought from discursive reason to poetry. And since some time in the sixteenth century Scotland has lacked such a language.

Every genuine literature, in other words, requires as its condition a means of expression capable of dealing with everything the mind can think or the imagination conceive. It must be a language for criticism as well as poetry, for abstract speculation as well as fact, and since we live in a scientific age, it must be a language for science as well. A language which can serve for one or two of those purposes but not for the others is, considered as a vehicle for literature, merely an anachronism. Scots has survived to our time as a language for simple poetry and the simpler kind of short story, such as *Thrawn Janet*; all its other uses have lapsed, and it expresses therefore only a fragment of the Scottish mind. One can go further than this, however, and assert that its very use is a proof that the Scottish consciousness is divided. For, reduced to its simplest terms, this linguistic division means that Scotsmen feel in one language and think in another; that their emotions turn to the Scottish tongue, with all its associations of local sentiment, and their minds to a standard English which for them is almost bare of associations other than those of the classroom. If Henryson and Dunbar had written prose they would have written in the same language as they used for poetry, for their minds were still whole; but Burns never thought of doing so, nor did Scott, nor did Stevenson, nor has any Scottish writer since. In an organic literature poetry is always influencing prose, and prose poetry; and their interaction energizes them both. Scottish poetry exists in a vacuum; it neither acts on the rest of literature nor reacts to it; and consequently it has shrunk to the level of anonymous folk-song. Hugh MacDiarmid has recently tried to revive it by impregnating it with all the contemporary influences of Europe one after another, and thus galvanize it into life by a series of violent shocks. In carrying out this experiment he has written some remarkable poetry; but he has left Scottish verse very much where it was before. For the major forms of poetry rise from a collision between emotion and intellect on a plane where both meet on equal terms; and it can never come into existence where the poet feels in one language and thinks in another, even though he should subsequently translate his thoughts into the language of his feelings. Scots poetry can only be revived, that is to say, when Scotsmen begin to think *naturally* in Scots. The curse of Scottish literature is the lack of a whole language, which finally means the lack of a whole mind.

This division in the Scottish consciousness is so far-reaching that if I were to enumerate all its consequences this chapter would go on to the end of the book. So I shall confine myself to some of its effects on poetry. I have often wondered why the Scots, who have shown themselves in the past to be a theological and speculative race, should have produced scarcely a single verse of good religious or metaphysical poetry. In the seventeenth century Scotland was steeped in theology far more thoroughly than England. Yet England produced the religious and metaphysical poetry of that time, and against Donne, Marvell, Traherne, Vaughan, Herbert and Crashaw, all that Scotland could show was a metrical version of the Psalms which is a curiosity.

Now it is clear that there are other reasons for this poverty of Scots poetry in the seventeenth century and since than the fact that Scotsmen already felt in one language and thought in another, and that there was no effective collaboration between their sensibility and their intellect. It will be best, therefore, to consider some of these reasons first. One of them was without doubt the strict Calvinism of the Scots, which was adverse both to the production of poetry, and to poetry itself. Another was the complete prohibition put upon poetic drama by the Reformers just when it seemed on the point of developing; a prohibition which killed not only the drama itself, but also a great number of other forms of poetry which normally flow from it. This matter of dramatic poetry, indeed, or rather the lack of it, was probably crucial for Scottish literature; and if that is so, then the Reformation truly signalized the beginning of Scotland's decline as a civilized nation. For poetic drama occupies a central and decisive position in the development of the three literatures which I mentioned at the beginning of this essay. In all three, English, French and German, poetry and literature in general came to self-consciousness in a great burst of poetic drama, and this achievement of self-consciousness influenced all the poetry that followed, whether lyrical or dramatic: poetry was thenceforth more aware of itself and more capable of essaying the non-dramatic major forms. If one compares the lyrical poetry of England before Shakespeare, of France before Racine, and of Germany before Goethe, with the lyrical poetry after them, one can see quite clearly this difference in self-consciousness. Before the change one finds the simple lyric with all its natural thoughtless grace; after it one finds a body of poetry lyrical in form, but expressing all the richness and complexity of experience as it is known to the self-perusing mind. To take a simple instance, the English metaphysical poetry of the sixteenth century with its "dialogue of one" would be inconceivable without the rich dramatic "dialogue of many" which preceded it or was contemporaneous with it.

The strict surveillance of Calvinism, then, and the consequent failure of Scotland to achieve poetic drama, may partly account for the fact that in her poetry since the sixteenth century she has failed to rise above the level of the simple lyric; why she has no Donne, no Baudelaire, no Hölderlin; why she has no romantic poet even of the rank of Beddoes; and why the only poetry with which hers can be compared is early medieval poetry such as that of Walter von der Vogelweide, and the folk-song which belongs indiscriminately to all peoples.

Yet allowing for Calvinism and the failure to achieve poetic drama, we do not completely account for the poverty and simplicity of Scottish poetry since the sixteenth century, for at the time when Scotland had a homogeneous literary language — when thought and feeling, in other words, could come to equal collision in the poet's mind — she did produce one major poem,

Henryson's "Testament of Cresseid", and a number of poems by such writers as Scott and Montgomery and the anonymous authors of the lyrics in the Bannatyne and Maitland collections, which in their intricacy of movement and fusion of feeling and thought foreshadowed the English metaphysicals. Take this verse from one of Alexander Scott's lyrics:

> Luve is ane fervent fire,
> Kendillit without desire:
>   Short plesour, lang displesour,
> Repentance is the hire;
>   Ane puir tressour without mesour:
> Luve is ane fervent fire.

Then take this from one of Burns's songs:

> But a' the pleasures e'er I saw,
>   Tho' three times doubl'd fairly,
> That happy night was worth them a',
>   Amang the rigs o' barley.

The first of these verses is written by a man who thinks and feels with equal intensity, on the same plane and in the same language, so that the thought heightens the feeling and the feeling the thought; while the second is a mere effusion of thoughtless emotion, with a commonplace judgment tagged on to it exalting feeling at the expense of everything else. If Burns had wished to express his real judgment on that night among the rigs of barley he would have turned to English, as he did in *Tam o' Shanter* in the one passage where he makes a serious reflection on life. Everybody knows it:

> But pleasures are like poppies spread,
> You seize the flow'r, its bloom is shed;
> Or like the snow falls in the river,
> A moment white—then melts for ever;
> Or like the Borealis race,
> That flit ere you can point their place;
> Or like the rainbow's lovely form
> Evanishing amid the storm.

I had often wondered why Burns suddenly dropped into English at this point, and for a long time I put down the whole passage as an unaccountable blemish, until I saw that it was the touch that made the poem perfect, the one serious reference that gave all the rest proportion. The point to be noticed, however, is that when Burns applied thought to his theme he turned to English. The reflection in this passage is neither deep nor original, but in the context it is quite adequate. And it is clear that Burns felt he could not express it in Scots, which was to him a language for sentiment but not for thought. He had no language which could serve him equally for both.

When emotion and thought are separated, emotion becomes irresponsible and thought arid. When they are separated so radically that they require two separate languages to express them, the first takes on very much the aspect of an indulgence and the second of disapproval. Scottish poetry is therefore largely emotion, and Scottish criticism has been until quite recent and degenerate times largely condemnation. They are alike in this, that they are equally without standards; for where poetry is written in a variety of dialects with no central language as a point of reference, it is impossible to evolve a criterion of style (there is no standard of Scots poetic style); and where criticism is divorced from sensibility, and consists in the mere elaboration or application of theories, it would in any case fail to judge poetry on genuine literary principles, even if such a criterion existed. Criticism, like poetry, requires a union of emotion and intellect, and where that union is broken criticism comes off as badly as poetry itself. So that in both provinces the division in the Scots mind and the Scots language has had disastrous effects. The worst thing that can be said about Scottish poetry and Scottish criticism is that they never come together, either in general or in the mind of the writer. And until Scotland has a common language for its prose and poetry, its thought and feeling, this evil must continue.

2. CRITICISM

Criticism is a customary and vital function of literature. A busy unofficial criticism went on, as we know, in the Elizabethan age. There was a still busier criticism in France in the time of Racine. And the great era of German literature was inaugurated by a very brilliant critic, Lessing, to whom Goethe afterwards so often expressed his gratitude. Of the most intimate and valuable kind of criticism it may be said that it is almost as much a function of language as of literature. The English criticism of the sixteenth and seventeenth centuries was deeply concerned with language; and so was the French. That is easy to understand; for no one can judge a work of literature unless he can use, and use expertly, the language in which it is written. And he can use expertly only the language in which he is accustomed to think, to feel and to write. A critic's main qualification consists in a sensitive but above all active understanding of the problems his writer is dealing with; he must not only be aware of these problems; he must also have had some positive experience of dealing with similar ones; and his attitude is more akin to collaboration than to fault-finding. This is to say that almost all good critics have been imaginative writers, and that the best have been poets: that is, men with a peculiarly intimate knowledge of the secrets and the possibilities of language.

Now it is clear that here Scottish criticism is in a peculiar and indeed invidious position. A Scottish writer dealing with the poetry of Burns in English is clearly not fulfilling the same function as Coleridge did when he dealt with the poetry of Shakespeare and Wordsworth. For between Burns and this writer, though both are Scotsmen, there is a barrier of speech. The critic cannot use Burns's language; he has no working standard, therefore, for measuring the excellence which Burns attained in it; but, most important of all, he is not in the least involved in the preservation of a living speech. All criticism of Burns is consequently at best what is called academic criticism: it never gets to grips with the subject.

What is the result? If criticism is not a vital function of the language it is dealing with, if it has no standard for measuring whether that language is being employed with excellence or merely with ordinary efficiency, if it always remains outside the province it is dealing with, what is left for it to judge? Little more than the obvious properties, the thoughts and feelings in a work; the qualities that might reach us through a good translation; the emotions which a man who loves music, but is not a musician, might derive from hearing a composition by Beethoven or Mozart. These emotions may be of the utmost interest and value, and they are legitimate matter for consideration: interesting books about Dostoevsky, for example, have been written by critics who could not read Russian, who were quite unaware that Dostoevsky wrote featureless prose but magnificent dialogue (a fact for which I am indebted to Prince D. M. Mirsky's *History of Russian*

Literature), and who had no possibility whatever of judging Dostoevsky from a literary point of view. Now such criticism is not without use, but to compare it with Coleridge's criticism of Shakespeare, which was the result of the most close communion between the critic's mind and the poet's through the medium of a single language in which both were in their different ways incomparably expert, is to feel how far it falls short of the complete and uncrippled exercise of the critical function. There is no apparatus in Scottish criticism, for example, for dealing with such a line as

> And peace proclaims olives of endless age,

whose virtue does not consist in the feelings and the thoughts it conveys, but in something else which is essential to poetry, and to poetry alone. It may be objected that this is because there are few such lines in the whole of Scottish poetry; but to that the reply is that such lines are only found in a literature where the critical intelligence, both in general and in the poet himself, is highly developed, and in a literature where all the resources of language, and not only a few, are at the poet's command. The greatest passages in English poetry, those in which we no longer seek for the ideas or the feelings expressed, but for something transcending them, could only have been written in a language which was employed for all the purposes of expression; for only by such employment does a language gather the requisite fullness and variety of association which make such feats possible. A language which is used only for poetry is bound to grow poorer, even for poetic purposes, than one which is used for all the ends of discourse. And a language which is not used for all those ends cannot be used critically, for such criticism as it receives is from outside, and is nothing more than an observer's opinion, of no real use.

This, it seems to me, is a fair description of the critical dilemma in Scotland: a dilemma caused by the fact that the critic uses one language and the poet another. There is no standard of criticism of Scots verse higher than the newspaper standard, which means that there is none at all. Poems are praised for their sentiments or their ideas, that is, for the same reasons as an uneducated reader praises some effusion in a local paper.

Now it is clear that this state of things constitutes a palpable danger to Scottish poetry; for one of its consequences is that anyone who writes Scots verse with any skill at all is greeted with approval, and not merely local approval, but general critical approval; and as long as that happens excellence has little chance of recognition. But the danger to the young Scottish poet is still greater. For not only will he get no help from outside, but he will find the general dilemma of criticism duplicated within himself. Having written a poem in Scots he will have no choice afterwards but to criticize it in English, and if he is honest he will probably have to admit that he is incapable of judging it. Where a poet thinks and feels in the same language, his thought enters in the closest way into the actual process of composition, becoming an organic part of it; for in all writing, whether in poetry or prose, criticism is a constant, even if sometimes unconscious, activity. It is shown in the mere act of discrimination, in the choice and arrangement of words. Yet though criticism is exercised in all writing, there is as much difference between its perfect and its imperfect use as there is between the greatest lines of Shakespeare and a business communication composed in an acquired tongue. Even a man who writes in one language and thinks in another, then, has a certain critical supervision over what he is writing; but it is only a rough-and-ready supervision; the action of his intelligence is not contemporaneous with his feeling: it is action at a distance. And if he should feel very strongly in the language he is employing, as he is likely to do if he is a Scotsman using Scots, the impetuous rush of feeling will be too strong for his mind to deal with it all at once; a torrent of emotions which he would never have expressed if his intellect had been in command will escape him; and he will find himself pouring out with a good conscience a perfect flood of sentimentality or of bombast. Any emotion which cannot be tested and passed by the mind of the man who feels it is sentimental: I am indebted for this generalization to a friend of mine, now dead, who never put it into writing. And Scottish poetry is, in proportion to its size, peculiarly rich in sentimentality, and when that fails, in bombast. I have tried to find an explanation for this, since some explanation is necessary; for the Scottish people are not themselves peculiarly sentimental or bombastic. The explanation is that, where the mind is divorced from the feelings so decisively that each uses a language of its own, the one can exercise only a very imperfect influence on the other.

The usual defence of Scots poetry is that it is lyrical, and that all poetry should be lyrical, should be as spontaneous as a song. That is in the last resort the critical standard on which all Scots poetry is judged. Now there is a theory to the effect that all poetry is by its nature lyrical, and that its true mark is a sort of spontaneity. A book like this is no place to enter into such a delicate question; and all that I shall try to establish is a fairly simple distinction. When one says that poetry is lyrical and spontaneous one makes a statement about the quality of poetry, not about its form. If that statement is true, as I believe it to be, then it is just as true of the texture of a vast intellectual construction such as *The Divine Comedy* or *Paradise Lost* as of a simple folk-song; for we are dealing with an essential property of all poetry. But if one means by the same statement that poetry must be simple and unambiguous both in quality and form, then one restricts poetry to the short lyric of sentiment and passion, and excludes most of what the world has agreed to call major poetry. By the same standard one would confine all music to melody; for the dramatic tragedy and the epic are roughly to the lyric what the symphony and the sonata are to the melody. Everybody would agree that Beethoven's music and Dante's poetry have a definite intellectual structure, and that they have at the same time a fundamental quality which is also present in the simple melody and the simple lyric, a quality which one may call, for lack of a better word, spontaneity. This quality is probably beyond analysis: it is related on the one hand to the Imagination as Coleridge conceived it, the Imagination in which all opposites are resolved, and on the other hand to what Coleridge called the sense of musical delight, for rhythm is essential to it. Poetry is not spontaneous in the sense that it is restricted to the expression of simple and spontaneous feelings, but rather in the sense that it reconciles the antitheses of feeling and thought into a harmony, achieving with apparent effortlessness a resolution of subject-matter which to the ratiocinative mind is known only as a difficulty to be overcome by intense effort. It was something like this that Schiller must have meant when he said that all art takes the form of play.

This, then, it seems to me, is the only valid sense in which poetry can be called lyrical, for the generalization applies to all poetry. But it can also be interpreted in a narrower way, and made to signify that all poetry should be simple and passionate, and that the intellect should have as little as possible to do with it. This interpretation is still, for all practical purposes, the Scottish one. Even admirers of Hugh MacDiarmid praise him chiefly for his first two books of lyrics, whereas easily his most original poetry is to be found in the long semi-philosophical poem, *A Drunk Man Looks At The Thistle.* They praise his lyrics at the expense of his poetry because they think that poetry should be simple and spontaneous, because there is an admirable canon of Scottish song in the simpler mode, by keeping to which one cannot go far wrong, or indeed far in any direction, and finally because their emotions speak one language and their minds another. If the English were to judge all their poetry by that, say, of Campion, they would be using a standard roughly resembling that which is used for Scots poetry indiscriminately. The result is that a really original Scots poet like Hugh MacDiarmid has never received in Scotland any criticism of his more ambitious poems which can be of the slightest use to him.

These are the evils, then, that flow from a radical division between sensibility and thought: first, a lack of intimacy in criticism, and secondly, a partiality for the simple unforced lyric, for all that is simple, which leaves out of account most of major poetry and major literature. Lacking intimacy, criticism of this kind takes on the floating opinions of its age, and makes of these a criterion for judging literature, both new and old. The Edinburgh reviewers of a century ago, Jeffrey, Lockhart and Wilson, lived in an era of dogmatic controversy, and so they were the "This will never do" type of critic. Our own age is one of unparalleled uncertainty about many things, of licentious opinion, and so Scottish criticism has swung round to the other extreme, to what might be called the "Anything will do" school. In the hands of this school Scottish criticism, lacking either sensibility or a standard, has become a mixture of Nationalist ideology, local patriotism and vague international sentiment, so that it has little relation to the writers it criticizes, who are at best a springboard to something else and more exciting. Such is Scottish criticism; without standards, sensibility, or even common sense; more like a disease of literature than a corrective. I have tried to analyse some of its causes and thus explain it. To justify it would be beyond the skill of any writer.

3. COMPARATIVE

I have attempted to show that there is a marked difference between Scottish poetry before and after the dissolution of Scots as a homogeneous literary language. To bring out this difference only examples will serve, and roughly parallel examples, if they could be found, would clearly be best of all. But unfortunately these parallels do not always exist, for there were kinds of poetry essayed in the autonomous phase of Scottish literature which have never been attempted since. We shall simply have to accept this fact.

I shall begin by taking a passage from Dunbar in his aureate style:

> Right as the stern of day begouth to shine,
> When gone to bed were Vesper and Lucine,
>   I raise and by a rosier did me rest;
> Up sprang the golden candle matutine
> With clear depurit beamis crystalline,
>   Glading the merry fowlis in their nest;
>   Or Phoebus was in purpur cape revest
> Up raise the lark, the heavenis ministrel fine,
>   In May, in-till a morrow mirthfullest.
>
> Full angel-like thir birdis sang their houris
> Within their courtens green in-to their bouris,
>   Apparelit white and red, with bloomis sweet;

Enamelit was the field with all colouris,
The pearly droppis shake in silver shouris,
  While all in balm did branch and leavis flete;
To part fra Phoebus, did Aurora greet,
her crystal tearis I saw hing on the flouris,
  Whilk he for luve all drank up with his heat.

For mirth of May, with skippis and with hoppis,
The birdis sang upon the tender croppis
  With curious note, as Venus chapel-clerkis:
The roses young new spreading of their knoppis,
Were powderit bricht with heavenly beriall droppis,
  Throw beamis red birning as ruby sparkis;
  The skies rang for shouting of the larkis,
The purpour heaven our-scailit in silver sloppis,
  Our-gilt the treis, branchis, leavis and barkis.

Doun throw the ryss ane river ran with streamis,
So lustily agane thae likand leamis,
  That all the lake as lamp did leam of licht,
Whilk shadowit all about with twinkling gleamis,
The bewis bathit were in second beamis
  Through the reflex of Phoebus' visage bricht.
  On every side the hedges raise on hicht,
The bank was green, the brook was full of bremis,
  The stanneris clear as stern in frosty nicht.

Now there is nothing in dialect Scottish poetry to correspond with this beautifully patterned and figured verse; and the only conclusion one can come to is that dialect Scots cannot rise to it, and is incongruous with it. In form Burns's *The Cottar's Saturday Night* comes closest to it, for the Spenserian stanza is the most ambitious that has ever been attempted in dialect Scots. But how can one compare a passage like the following with Dunbar's poetry?

> The cheerfu' supper done, wi' serious face,
> They, round the ingle, form a circle wide;
> The sire turns o'er, with patriarchal grace,
> The big ha'-bible, ance his father's pride:
> His bonnet rev'rently is laid aside,
> His lyart haffets wearing thin and bare;
> Those strains that once did sweet in Zion glide,
> He wales a portion with judicious care;
> And 'Let us worship God!' he says with solemn air.

Considering these two passages, several things become clear at once. First of all, the immense loss in technical skill which Scottish poetry suffered between Dunbar and Burns, the loss of the whole *art* of poetry. Dunbar was, technically, quite as skilful a poet as Spenser, though a far less great one, for he never rises to the height of

> O! turn thy rudder hitherward awhile,
> Here may thy storm-bett vessel safely ryde,
> This is the Port of Rest from troublous toyle,
> The worldes sweet In from pain and wearisome turmoyle.

lines which may have suggested Milton's still greater ones in *Paradise Regained*:

> I would be at the worst; worst is my Port,
> My harbour and my ultimate repose.

The difference in practical effect between Dunbar's skill as a poet and Spenser's is that Dunbar's led to nothing very much, whereas Spenser's was incorporated into the body of English poetry, was taken up by Marlowe and through Marlowe led on to Shakespeare and Milton, and two centuries later could help to form the genius of Keats and Tennyson. This mere skill in Scottish poetic art, then, fell into a sort of bottomless gap after the Reformation and the events that inevitably followed it; and finally it lacked even a language which could perpetuate it. For all essential purposes it was lost. One cannot believe that Dunbar could have written

> The cheerfu' supper done, wi' serious face,
> They, round the ingle, form a circle wide.

The technique of poetry in his time was too high to have passed such lines as these. That Burns is a greater poet than Dunbar does not affect this argument, except to strengthen it.

The second thing that must strike anyone reading these two passages is that Dunbar is writing in a self-subsistent language and that Burns is writing in a sort of ragtag of phrases, neither ordinary speech nor poetic diction, but an arbitrary amalgam of both. Dunbar and Spenser would never have thought of furnishing a "sire" with "lyart haffets". The whole passage, indeed, is false both in feeling and style, for Burns is thinking in English and introducing a Scots word now and then, and his confusion is plain.

The third thing that becomes clear when we examine *The Cottar's Saturday Night* is that dialect Scots is not equal to the strain put upon it by the Spenserian stanza; indeed Burns admitted this by finishing up in pure English, for the last half of the poem is undisguisedly in that tongue. But even where he sticks to dialect Scots, how much of the flavour of it is lost in its ambitious surroundings:

> November chill blaws loud wi' angry sugh;
> The short'ning winter-day is near a close;
> The miry beasts retreating frae the pleugh;
> The black'ning trains o' craws to their repose:
> The toil-worn Cottar frae his labour goes,—
> This night his weekly moil is at an end,
> Collects his spades, his mattocks and his hoes,
> Hoping the morn in ease and rest to spend,
> And weary, o'er the moor, his course does homeward bend.

Compare that with

> O merry hae I been teethin' a heckle,
> And merry hae I been shapin' a spoon;
> And merry hae I been cloutin' a kettle,
> And kissin' my Katie when a' was done.
> O a' the lang day I ca' at my hammer,
> An' a' the lang day I whistle and sing,
> A' the lang night I cuddle my kimmer,
> An' a' the lang night as happy's a king.

It is the difference between forced, concocted rhyming and poetry.

Fergusson also attempted ambitious forms in dialect Scots, and succeeded better than Burns, for he was a more scrupulous artist and he used a more organic language:

> The fient a cheep's amang the bairnies now;
>   For a' their anger's wi' their hunger gane:
> Ay maun the childer, wi' a fastin' mou',
>   Grumble and greet, and mak an unco mane.
> In rangles round, before the ingle's lowe,
>   Frae Gudame's mouth auld-warld tales they hear,
> O' warlocks loupin' round the wirrikow:
>   O' ghaists that win in glen and kirkyard drear,
> Whilk touzles a' their tap, and gars them shak wi' fear!

Fergusson's use of dialect Scots was infinitely more close and workmanlike than Burns's, as this passage shows; one feels, indeed, that had he lived he might have contrived, with his genius for words, to turn dialect Scots into a literary language; for it is evident from his poetry, as from no other Scottish dialect poetry except the Ballads, that he is thinking in terms of the language he uses. But he died when he was twenty-three; and dialect Scots has never been used with equal solidity and exactitude and deliberate mastery since. *The Farmer's Ingle* is, in any case, a far better poem than *The Cottar's Saturday Night*, which is roughly upon the same theme. The two poems, indeed, furnish excellent examples of the genuine and the false use of language.

My second quotation is from a kind of poetry in which both classical Scots and dialect Scots excelled: that is the lyric. Here is an anonymous poem from the Bannatyne

MS., which dates from 1568, but according to Miss M. M. Gray in her excellent anthology, *Scottish Poetry from Barbour to James VI*, "includes poems nearly two centuries older". It seems to me one of the supreme lyrics in Scottish literature.

My heart is heigh above,
   My body is full of bliss,
For I am set in luve,
   As weil as I wald wiss;
I luve my lady pure,
   And she luvis me again;
I am her serviture,
   She is my souverane.

She is my very heart,
   I am her hope and heal;
She is my joy inwart,
   I am her luvar leal;
I am her bound and thrall,
   She is at my command;
I am perpetual
   Her man, both fute and hand.

The thing that may her please
   My body sall fulfil;
Whatever her disease,
   It dois my body ill.
My bird, my bonnie ane,
   My tender babe venust,
My luve, my life alane,
   My liking and my lust.

We interchange our hairtis
In otheris armis soft;
Spreitless we twa depairtis
Usand our luvis oft;
We murne when licht day dawis,
We plain the nicht is short,
We curse the cock that crawis,
That hinderis our disport.

I glowffin up agast,
When I her miss on nicht,
And in my oxter fast
I find the bowster richt;
Then langour on me lies,
Like Morpheus the mair,
Whilk causes me uprise
And to my sweet repair:

And then is all the sorrow
Furth of remembrance,
That ever I had aforrow
In luvis observance.
Thus never do I rest,
So lusty a life I lead,
When that I list to test
The well of womanheid.

Luvaris in pain, I pray
God send you sic remead
As I have nicht and day,
You to defend from deid;

Therefore be ever true
  Unto your ladies free,
And they will on you rue,
  As mine has done on me.

Burns has written some of the most beautiful love songs in the Scots language, and his greatness is shown in their immense variety. The poem which corresponds most closely in mood to the poem I have just quoted is one of his best known. Nevertheless I must quote it for the sake of comparison.

O, my luve's like a red, red rose,
  That's newly sprung in June:
O, my luve's like the melodie
  That's sweetly played in tune.

As fair art thou, my bonnie lass,
  So deep in luve am I;
And I will luve thee still, my dear,
  Till a' the seas gang dry.

Till a' the seas gang dry, my dear,
  And the rocks melt wi' the sun:
And I will luve thee still, my dear,
  While the sands o' life shall run.

And fare thee well, my only luve!
  And fare thee well a while!
And I will come again, my luve,
  Though it were ten thousand mile.

These two poems are each perfect in its own way; they are both passionate, simple and direct; yet the first seems to me to belong to a different world of poetry from the second, and a far more satisfying one. By this I do not mean merely that Burns's song is folk-poetry and the other what the Germans call *Kunst*, or art-poetry, though that is obvious; for this poem could only have been written in an age when a high standard of poetical performance existed, when, in other words, there was a sensitive critical audience for poetry. I mean rather that there is something in the very substance of the first which is lacking in the second, something which was lost to Scottish poetry after the sixteenth century and has never been recovered since: a quality which might be called wholeness. Burns's poem is pure sentiment, sentiment at its very best, but nothing more. The earlier poem has sentiment too, but it is ennobled and transformed by something which Burns could not know, for the Scotland of his day did not know it: that is a philosophy of life and following from that a philosophy of love which accounted for all the aspects of love, sensual, romantic and spiritual, so that all three could be given their due force in one poem with perfect balance and propriety. One way of saying this is that in addition to its other beauties the earlier poem has an intellectual beauty which transfigures the feeling on all its planes. Even the appeal to God in the last verse is merely a pròof of the completeness of the poet's response to the experience he is dealing with; it does not strike us in the least as incongruous, and it is not sentimental, as Burns's similar appeals always were. This poem is both more exalted and more earthly than the Scottish lyric has ever been since; and if I were asked to give some proof of the enormous loss which Scotland sustained when its literary tradition was broken I should only have to point to it. I have no wish to deny Burns's genius, the greatest individual genius in Scottish poetry. But he appeared at a time when the tradition of Scottish poetry was dead, and he did not have a language which could express what is expressed in this beautiful poem.

This poem has an intellectual content, and contains the seed from which a metaphysical poetry might have grown. In the next two poems the intellectual power is considerably more evident, and there is consequently nothing at all in post-Reformation poetry with which to compare them. They represent a quality in Scottish poetry which has been lost for good, a quality which has not even been striven for since, even unsuccessfully. The first is another anonymous poem from the Bannatyne MS.:

Luve has me wardit in ane park of pain,
With dolour is the double dykis dicht,
And lust is forster with his bow and flane;
Fro tree to tree he chasis me in the nicht.
I weep, I wring, was never ane wearier wicht,
Thus nicht and day with piteous voice I cry;
Was never ane under the sunnis licht
Mair patient sufferit proctory.

Wald ye send help soon with ane spade of hope,
And cast the dyke of dolour to the erd,

With lusty hairt then suld I give ane lope
And come to you, I ken the gait unspeired,
My hairt is youris, full steidfastly, unsteired.
Fetterit full fast whill ye mak it free.
I send till you most fairest on this erd
Mo commendationnis with humilitie.

The second is by Alexander Scott, whose poetry was also written before 1568:

Lo! what it is to luve,
Learn ye, that list to pruve,
Be me, I say, that no wayis may
The grund of grief remuve,
Bot still decay, both nicht and day:
Lo! what it is to luve.

Luve is ane fervent fire,
Kendillit without desire:
Short plesour, lang displesour,
Repentance is the hire;
Ane puir tressour without mesour:
Luve is ane fervent fire.

To luve and to be wise,
To rege with gude advice,
Now thus, now than, so goes the game,
Incertain is the dice:
There is no man, I say, that can
Both luve and to be wise.

> Flee alwayis from the snare;
> Learn at me to be ware;
> It is ane pain and double trane
> Of endless woe and care;
> For to refrain that danger plain,
> Flee alwayis from the snare.

In these two poems we have passion and passionate reflection on passion, and in the second one — what follows from the subtler reaches of reflection — a form that suits its windings, a form at once simple and intricate. We never have this union of passion and reflection in folk poetry, or, so far as I know, in dialect poetry; partly perhaps because poor and hard-working people have no leisure for it, and partly because dialect is not capable of the more exalted forms of reflection, expressing as it does everyday and local needs. Dialect and folk-poetry is rich enough in general reflections of the proverbial kind, that is, reflections *on* experience; but what the poetry I have just quoted gives us is reflection that deals in the most intimate way with experience from inside, decisively modifying and enriching it. This enrichment of experience is as good a criterion of civilization as one could find; and by the evidence of Alexander Scott's poetry it is clear that the most sensitive and intelligent classes in Scotland were far more civilized four hundred years ago than they are now. For this kind of poetry must have had a contemporary audience which understood it and appreciated it; and that means that for some time towards the end of the pre-Reformation Age there must have existed in Scotland a high culture of the feelings as well as of the mind: a concord which was destroyed by the rigours of Calvinism, so that hardly a trace of it has been left. What took its place was either simple irresponsible feeling side by side with arid intellect, or else that reciprocally destructive confrontation of both for which Gregory Smith found the name of "the Caledonian Antisyzygy": a recognition that they are irreconcilable, and that Scottish life is split in two beyond remedy. That Scottish life is split in two is certain; it is my main argument in this essay. But that it has always been split in two is false, as is proved by the poetry I have just quoted; and that it should be split in two, as Hugh MacDiarmid seems to claim in his essay on the Caledonian Antisyzygy, is a theory which not even the intellect can sustain. The mere assertion of life in its most simple form is an act of reconciliation. And the mark of great poetry, as Coleridge has said, is that it reconciles all opposites in a harmony. If Scottish poetry is doomed for ever to express this Antisyzygy, then it contains no principle of progress, no dialectic, to use the fashionable cant term, and must remain stationary. It has done so since its first brilliant flowering.

The last three poems which I have quoted are marked by that union of feeling and intellect which I have tried to show can only be achieved in a homogeneous literary language. They are all lyrical. But there is another kind of poem which also requires a homogeneous literary language as its condition: the semi-dramatic narrative poem. Scottish literature can show one great example in this kind: Henryson's *Testament of Cresseid*. This poem is so well known that only the necessity for comparison induces me to quote from it. The first passage describes how Troilus, riding back to Troy long after his disastrous love for Cresseid, passes her, now a leper, begging by the wayside:

> Then upon him she cast up baith her ene,
> And with ane blenk it come into his thocht
> That he sometime her face befoir had sene;
> But she was in sic ply he knew her nocht;
> Yet then her look into his mind it brocht
> The sweet visage and amorous blenking
> Of fair Cresseid, sometime his awin darling.

The second passage contains Henryson's epitaph on the story, his poetic judgment:

> Some said he made ane tomb of marble gray,
> And wrote her name and superscriptioun,
> And laid it on her grave, where that she lay,
> In golden letteris, containing this reasoun:
> 'Lo, fair ladies, Cresseid of Troyis toun,
> Sometime countit the flour of womanheid,
> Under this stane, late leper, lyis deid.'

Now this again is poetry requiring a union of emotion and intellect, of passion and judgment at their highest reach; and it could only have been written in a language which the poet used for both purposes. It is the kind of poetry which in any other country would have found its final expression in poetic tragedy: but the rule of the Reformers, as we know, wrecked any chance of that development. The only post-Reformation poem with which we can compare or contrast it is *Tam o' Shanter*, the second greatest narrative poem in Scottish literature. The difference between these two works is the difference which I have been trying to emphasize throughout this essay: that between work governed by the intellect and work untouched by it. *Tam o' Shanter* is a brilliant poem, superb in its humorous fantasy and its energy; and taking it for what it is intended to be, it could not be better. But it is in a different class from *The Testament of Cresseid*, and also in the only class which dialect Scots has been able to achieve in narrative poetry since the breakdown of the major Scots tradition. *Bonny Kilmeny* also belongs to this class: that of wild irresponsible fantasy ungoverned by intellect. I am not arguing here against this kind of poetry, for *Tam o' Shanter* is certainly a masterpiece of its kind. I merely wish to show that classical Scots was capable of producing certain kinds of poetry which dialect Scots has never attempted, and of which I believe it to be, by virtue of its limitations, incapable. These kinds of poetry all presuppose a homogeneous language capable of expressing all that a people has the ability or the wish to express, on all the levels of thought and feeling, and of thought combined with feeling; and without such a language the consciousness of a people is crippled.

I have quoted enough to show what Scotland lost with the loss of its language. But I should like to give a few extracts from yet another poem, which seems to me one of the most beautiful in the Scots language, and foreshadows in the most curious way both Marvell and Wordsworth. It is *Of the Day Estivall*, by Alexander Hume, who was born round about 1550 and died in 1609.

> O perfite Light, whilk shed away
> The darkness from the light,
> And set a ruler owre the day,
> Ane other owre the night,

it begins. I shall quote only a verse here and there.

> The subtle mottie rayons bright
> At rifts they are in wonne,
> The glancing vanes and vitre bright
> Resplends against the sun. . . .
>
> Begaried is the sapphire pend
> With spraings of scarlet hue,
> And preciously from end till end
> Damasked white and blue. . . .
>
> All trees and simples great and small,
> That balmy leaf do bear,
> Nor they were painted on a wall
> Na mair they move or steir.
>
> Calm is the deep and purpour sea,
> Yea, smoother nor the sand;
> The wawis that welt'ring wont to be
> Are stable like the land.

Sa silent is the cessile air,
  That every cry and call,
The hills, the vales, the forest fair
  Again repeats them all. . . .

The herds beneath some leafy tree,
  Amids the flowers they lie;
The stable ships upon the sea
  Tends up their sails to dry. . . .

With gilded eyes and open wings,
  The cock his courage shaws,
With claps of joy his breast he dings,
  And twenty times he craws.

The dow with whistling wings sa blue,
  The winds can fast collect,
His purpour pennes turns mony hue
  Against the sun direct. . . .

Our west horizon circuler,
  Fra time the sun be set,
Is all with rubies (as it were)
  Of roses reid ourfret.

What pleasure were to walk and see,
  Endlang a river clear,
The perfite form of every tree
  Within the deep appear.

I have quoted only a few verses from this poem, but enough to show that in mood and style it foreshadows

Marvell in the most astonishing way. It is the only poem in Scots, so far as I know, which combines the two elements which make Marvell's poetry so lovely: that is a luxurious delight in Nature and a deep and sweet religious feeling. In it, as in the poems I have already quoted, we get one of those combinations of opposites which we never get again after the dissolution of the Scottish poetic tradition, a combination which in England produced not merely one poem but a whole school of poetry, in which Marvell, Traherne and Vaughan are the best-known names. After Hume we never find this union of natural and religious feeling in Scots poetry: religion is one thing, nature another, and there is no bridge between them: the Caledonian Antisyzygy sets in.

I shall conclude this brief survey with Mark Alexander Boyd's sonnet, which Mr Ezra Pound admires so much. Boyd died in 1601.

> Fra bank to bank, fra wood to wood I rin,
> Ourhailit with my feeble fantasie;
> Like til a leaf that fallis from a tree,
> Or til a reed ourblawin with the win.
> Twa gods guides me: the ane of tham is blin,
> Yea and a bairn brocht up in vanitie;
> The neist a wife ingenrit of the sea,
> And lichter nor a dauphin with her fin.
> Unhappy is the man for evermair
> That tills the sand and sawis in the air;
> But twice unhappier is he, I lairn,
> That feidis in his hairt a mad desire,
> And followis on a woman throw the fire,
> Led by a blind and teachit by a bairn.

Set these few scraps taken from the old poetry of Scotland against all that has been written in dialect Scots in the three and a half centuries since, and what comparison can there be? Consider also that a great deal of that old poetry has been irrecoverably lost; that in his *Lament for the Makars* Dunbar mentions twenty-two poets, most of them obviously contemporary with him, and that of these only four or five are known to us by their works. Consider the scope, the variety, the formal beauty, the high temper of the poetry which has come down to us from that time, and reflect what a loss Scotland suffered in losing its language and its civilization. The loss of civilization is bound up with the loss of language; for no civilization can exist without a speech in which it can express both its thought and its passion: without an adult tongue, for there can be no maturity except through a working relation between feeling and thought. Dialect is to a homogeneous language what the babbling of children is to the speech of grown men and women; it is blessedly ignorant of the wider spheres of thought and passion, and when it touches upon them its response is as irresponsible as that of the irremediably immature. Anyone, indeed, who chose to enter into this problem of Scottish dialect poetry from the psychological side, could make out a good case for the thesis that Scottish dialect poetry is a regression to childhood, an escape from the responsibility of the whole reason to the simplicity and irresponsibility of the infant mind. To most of us who were born and brought up in Scotland dialect Scots is associated with childhood, and English with maturity. This may be a regrettable fact, but it must be accepted; for there is no Scots language to which we can pass over from the restricted and local province of dialect: there is only English. When, therefore, having forsaken dialect speech and its associations of thought and feeling, we turn back to it again, we plunge in spite of ourselves into the simple world of childhood, with its emotions untouched by thought, its sanctioned irresponsibility and endless false hopes. I do not want to insist too much on this argument; yet if it is true it helps further to account for the simplicity of Scottish dialect poetry. In any case, compared with Scottish poetry since, that of the Makars is adult poetry.

I said a little while ago that Scotland's loss of a native civilization was bound up with its loss of a native language. This does not mean that it lost its civilization because it lost its language; to find the cause of both calamities one would have to delve into Scottish history, and, as history is very largely the product of character, into the Scottish character as well. I have no space in this short book for such an extensive undertaking, and shall content myself with a few general observations. When a nation loses its language it loses an essential unifying element in its life, and as soon as that happens the things which divide it begin to take precedence over the things which unite it. Surveying English literature, one would say that the English are a people to whom the things which unite them are of more importance than the things which divide them; and surveying Scottish literature, one would come to the exactly opposite conclusion. For a little while Scottish history shows us a rich and fertile cohesion, and that short age produced a brilliant literature. But just at the moment when this literature should have flowered most splendidly it was cut off, and that dissension arose which has troubled Scotland ever since, and has not yet been composed. If this is true, then it is not fair to say of Scotland in general that the things which divide it are of more importance than the things which unite it: for that is true historically only of Protestant Scotland. The Scotland of James IV shows us a coherent civilization, and in the individual writer thought and feeling harmoniously working together. Calvinism drove a wedge between these two things, and destroyed the language in which they had been fused. Dissension can take strange forms, and Calvinism was prolific in dissensions; and I think it is plausible to assert that the splitting up of the Scottish language into a host of local dialects was merely a final result of radical internal conflicts, civil and religious, working continuously for over a century. That conflict was so bitter and remorseless that it finally tore to pieces the living fabric of language itself, and left nothing but the shreds with which Scottish poetry has had to content itself since.

This is an inquiry into Scottish literature; and in writing of the loss of the Scottish language and civilization I have been concerned with its effects on Scottish literature. But it must obviously have had far more general effects as well, for such a catastrophe involves the whole of a people's existence from top to bottom.

> Things fall apart; the centre cannot hold;
> Mere anarchy is loosed upon the world,

Mr W. B. Yeats has written about our own time. We live in hope that the present state of the world will not be of century-long duration; and this makes it possible for us to bear it. But the centre has not held in Scotland for four hundred years; during all that time it has never been united, and the part has always meant more than the whole. A nation in which the mind is divorced from the feelings will act with hot savagery at times, and with chill insensibility at others; and the loss of Scottish civilization, of Scottish unity, is the only thing that can explain the peculiarly brutal form which the Industrial Revolution took in Scotland, where its chief agents are only conceivable as thoughtless or perverted children. No doubt the disunity of Scotland made it more favourable for the growth of Capitalism in the early stages of Capitalism; for then the very fact that every man was out for himself, the very fact that there was no effective community, was an actual advantage. It is since Capitalism reached what may be called its collective phase that Scotland has fallen behind as a capitalist country: there are other reasons for this as well, certainly, but this one should not be entirely lost sight of. What Scotland has suffered in the way of private and public lack of amenity, of household and official barbarity, by the loss of its civilization, it would be impossible for anyone to estimate. The destruction of a civilization and a literature is bound to draw other consequences behind it of far greater scope. But I am not concerned here with these: I can only indicate them and pass on.

The main point in all this inquiry so far — I must return

to it at the risk of appearing monotonous — is the crucial difference between a literature which has an autonomous language in which to express itself, and a literature which has to depend on a number of disconnected dialects. I have called this autonomous language Scots, and I am not concerned with its linguistic origins or correspondences. "Scottish was a development from Northern English," says Miss M. M. Gray in her anthology, "and, in the work of Barbour, the earliest Scottish poet, is but slightly differentiated from Northern English; the difference gradually increased." This, I have no doubt, is perfectly true. But it seems to me that the language of Scottish literature can only be called Scots, however nearly it may be related to Northern English. What other test except the literary test, indeed, can be applied to it, and what other importance except that it produced a literature can be attached to it? Its decisive importance is that it was a language, a uniting and overarching principle; and that Scotland has never had one since.

4. THE PLACE OF POETIC DRAMA

At an earlier stage in this essay I advanced the theory that poetic tragedy represents a crucial stage in the literature of a people, and that by means of it poetry becomes self-conscious, which is another way of saying that it becomes mature. I pointed to the literatures of England, France and Germany in justification of this generalization. It will be generally agreed that the greatest age in all three literatures was an age of poetic tragedy. Goethe held that poetic tragedy was the greatest of all literary forms, and considered the writing of it the highest activity of which any man was capable. I am not concerned with such speculations, however, but rather with the fact that poetic tragedy produces a change in any literature into which it enters, and that literature becomes a different thing after it from what it was before it.

Most of the poetry which precedes poetic drama is of three kinds, lyrical, didactic, and narrative. The first generally expresses a single emotion with the associations appropriate to it; the second is made up of moral reflections touched with feeling and sometimes interspersed with allegory; the third is frequently semi-dramatic, like Chaucer's *Troilus and Criseyde* and Henryson's *Testament of Cresseid*, but the narrator is always present as a directing agent, and the dramatic characters do not have complete independence in the working out of the action. Narrative poetry comprises some of the greatest that has ever been written, including that of Homer, Dante, Chaucer, Spenser, Milton and Wordsworth; and it would be idle to speculate whether it is or is not as great a form as poetic tragedy. Its scope is more extensive than poetic tragedy; like that it generally contains both dramatic and lyrical elements; but it may contain many others as well; it may be purely interesting or purely descriptive, point to a moral, invent fanciful episodes of no dramatic relevance, and use any device in general which comes under the category of story-telling. The historical importance of poetic tragedy is that it can do none of these things; that it confronts the poet immediately with a typical human situation, and compels him to work it out to an end. That situation is, by the very terms of poetic tragedy, a conflict, either a simple conflict between two definite opposing powers, or a complex one into which several powers enter; and the poet has to take every side in turn and state each with the utmost force and objectivity. This is never a cold and judicial act; it is much more like "a sustained passion of self-obliteration, through identification with the creatures of the imagination", to quote from Mr Middleton Murry's book on Shakespeare. That is to define the dramatic process too violently, however; but it is at least a process in which both the mind and the imagination are put to their utmost stretch in an objectivization of all the conflicting powers of the poet, not in peace or suspension, but in intense action. The result is a unique act of self-consciousness, perhaps the most comprehensive act of self-consciousness possible to the human mind outside of mystical contemplation. An act such as this changes the point of gravity of poetry; that is no longer the simple lyrical point, but rather a point determined by a balance between several contending orbits, each of which may be regarded as lyrical, each as a partial expression of the imagination, but given its place and its value in an action working towards an end. This act is, then, compared with simple lyrical utterance, an assertion of self-consciousness: it may even be, as Mr Middleton Murry says, a "spontaneous utterance of the undivided being". But that is not a question into which I can enter here, for this is not an inquiry into the nature of tragedy, but into the problem of Scottish literature; and all that I wish to bring out is that poetic tragedy marks a great increase of self-consciousness in any literature in which it appears, and that a literature which lacks it probably lacks something which is necessary for the supreme kinds of poetry.

As for what a literature loses by missing the phase of poetic tragedy, that is impossible to compute, and must depend largely on supposition. It is likely to lack metaphysical poetry, the "dialogue of one", and all the forms of poetry in which feeling is set against feeling and the intellect enters as a comparative or critical factor. It is also likely to lack a varied and comprehensive language. "We are to recollect," says Coleridge, "that the dramatist represents his characters in every situation of life and in every state of mind, and there is no form of language which may not be introduced by a great and judicious poet, and yet be most strictly according to nature." Coleridge pointed this out to refute "a general and mistaken notion that because some forms of writing and some combinations of thought are not usual, they are not natural"; but it has also another bearing, that is, on the vocabulary of poetry. Coleridge says that "there is no form of language which may not be introduced" by the dramatic poet; and it seems to me that this cannot be postulated of any other kind of poet, lyrical, didactic, or narrative. In the Elizabethan and Jacobean age the English language was employed for poetry with a flexibility and lavishness which it never achieved again, and which it cannot achieve in any age which lacks dramatic utterance. Yet the dramatic use of poetry by the Elizabethans also enriched the general vocabulary of English poetry, and made it an instrument for kinds of poetry which it could not have produced otherwise. This is a truism, but it is necessary to insist upon it in any consideration of Scottish poetry, which never knew this change at all. What we see in Scottish poetry after the sixteenth century is accordingly a gradual impoverishment of the vocabulary of poetry, an impoverishment which may be judged most clearly by comparing the language of Dunbar with that of Burns. The Scots speech not only became localized; it thinned to a trickle.

We cannot say now whether Scotland would have had a dramatic literature had the Reformation never taken place, or had it taken a different form. The only considerable example of dramatic art that has come down to us from the sixteenth century is Lyndsay's *Ane pleasant Satyre of the Three Estaitis*, which was first produced in

Cupar either in 1535 or 1540, and was afterwards presented in Linlithgow and Edinburgh. It is a morality play, containing such characters as King Humanity, Wantounness, Placebo, Sandie Solace, Flattrie, Chastitie, Divyne Correctioun, and so on; but the characters are drawn with great lifelikeness and spirit, and the dramatic skill of the whole is remarkable; for Lyndsay, though a mediocre poet, seems to have been an excellent play-wright. J. H. Millar, in his neglected *Literary History of Scotland* says, referring to this play: "In literature, as in politics, it may be that the 'might-have-beens' are illegitimate, as they are futile. But to wonder how the course of Scottish drama might have run if the external conditions had been analogous to those that prevailed in England is certainly a tempting, and perhaps after all an innocent, speculation. That these conditions were, unhappily, very different in the two countries is well known. The Reformation in England helped to pave the way for the Elizabethan drama. In Scotland it was hostile to almost every form of art, and fatal to that which finds its home on the stage. The old sports and pastimes of the people were suppressed with a heavy hand. 'Robert Hude', Lyttil Johne, the Abbot of Unreason, and the Quene of the May, were ostracized both in burgh and to landwart. For well-nigh a hundred and fifty years the desolating influence of a gloomy and intolerant fanaticism brooded over the country; and, while it permanently deprived the people of forms of amusement which might have developed into something really worth developing, it did little to abate the national appetite for drink and fornication. If we may judge by Lyndsay's *Satyre*, no nation could have shown a fairer promise of playing a worthy part in the dramatic revival which is the glory of English literature at the end of the sixteenth and the beginning of the seventeenth century." He praises Lyndsay for the dramatic propriety of the action in this play, and the vividness with which the characters are represented. This praise is reasonable, as well as the contention that miracle and morality plays must have been common in Scotland, though Lyndsay's *Satyre* is the only example that has survived, except for a brilliant fragment by Dunbar or some unknown hand. One can say, from the evidence of the *Satyre* and the correlative evidence, that the germ from which a drama might have sprung existed in Scotland. After the change represented by the Reformation that drama could not develop; if the Reformation had never happened it might have developed, or it might not: that is all that we can say about it. But in support of the first supposition can be advanced the strong gift for dramatic statement which is shown in another large sphere of Scottish literature: that is the Ballads. The best of the Scottish Ballads are more dramatic than the English, a fact which can probably be explained by the fact that the English dramatic sense found an outlet in a different and much more comprehensive form, and that the Scottish dramatic sense did not. The whole grammar of the greatest Scottish Ballads is dramatic, a sort of simplified question and answer. We come across it again and again. In *Clerk Saunders*:

'Is there ony room at your head, Saunders?
  Is there ony room at your feet?
Or ony room at your side, Saunders,
  Where fain, fain, I wad sleep?'

'There's nae room at my head, Margret,
  There's nae room at my feet;
My bed it is fu' lowly now,
  Amang the hungry worms I sleep.'

In *The Daemon Lover*:

'What hills are yon, yon pleasant hills,
  The sun shines sweetly on?'—
'O yon are the hills o' Heaven,' he said,
  'Where you will never won.'—

'O whaten-a mountain is yon?' she said,
  'Sae dreary wi' frost and snae?'—
'O yon is the mountain o' Hell,' he said,
  'Where you and I will gae.

'But haud your tongue, my dearest dear,
  Let a' your follies a-bee,
I'll show you where the white lilies grow,
  In the bottom o' the sea.'

In *The Lass of Lochroyan*:

'O wha will shoe my bonny foot?
  And wha will glove my hand?
And wha will bind my middle jimp
  W' a lang, lang linen band?

'O wha will kame my yellow hair,
With a haw bayberry kame?
And wha will be my babe's father
Till Gregory come hame?'—

'Thy father, he will shoe thy foot,
Thy brother will glove thy hand,
Thy mither will bind thy middle jimp
Wi' a lang, lang linen band.

'Thy sister will kame thy yellow hair,
Wi' a haw bayberry kame;
The Almighty will be thy babe's father
Till Gregory come hame.'

If I were to go on quoting, I should never stop. It is true, of course, that this method of question and answer is as much narrative as dramatic: in the last resort a means of telling a story. But though this is so, it has at its best a genuine dramatic power quite apart from its narrative intention, as in

I'll show you where the white lilies grow
In the bottom o' the sea,

and in

The Almighty will be thy babe's father
Till Gregory come hame.

I have said that there can be no dramatic poetry except in a language in which the poet can both think and feel, and the Ballads bear out this contention; for they are almost the only Scottish dialect poetry extant in which the poet both thinks and feels in the dialect he uses. Scottish folk-song is pure feeling; but the Ballads express a view of life which is essentially philosophic, though completely devoid of reflection. The dramatic apparatus in them is extremely simple and rudimentary, it is true, and capable of presenting only the most direct contrasts; but for its purpose it is perfectly effective. All that I wish to show, however, is that the disposition to dramatic presentation existed in Scotland on a general scale, and that it might plausibly have found utterance in poetic tragedy if the Reformers had not radically discouraged it. Scotland's dramatic power seems to have gone, in the seventeenth century, into controversy of the dullest but most violent kind, producing such monstrosities as *The Causes of the Lord's Wrath against Scotland, The Poor Man's Cup of Cold Water*, and *Eleven Points to bind up a Believer's Breeches*. In such conflicts there is no catharsis, and no making towards a unity: there is mere division, and nothing but division.

5. FANTASY

In G. Gregory Smith's preciose but sensible book, *Scottish Literature: Character and Influence*, there's a passage which has now become famous. Speaking of the "shortness and cohesion" of Scottish literature, he says that that literature is nevertheless "remarkably varied and that it becomes, under the stress of foreign influence and native division and reaction, almost a zigzag of contradictions. The antithesis need not, however, disconcert us. Perhaps in the very combination of opposites — what either of the two Sir Thomases, of Norwich and Cromarty, might have been willing to call 'the Caledonian Antisyzygy' — we have a reflection of the contrasts which the Scot shows at every turn, in his political and ecclesiastical history, in his polemical restlessness, in his adaptability, which is another way of saying that he has made allowance for new conditions, in his practical judgment, which is the admission that two sides of the matter have been considered. If therefore Scottish history and life are, as an old northern writer said of something else, 'varied with a clean contrair spirit', we need not be surprised to find that in his literature the Scot presents two aspects which appear contradictory."

Gregory Smith goes on from this point to define two "moods" in Scottish literature. I shall quote his own definition of them.

"One characteristic mood stands out clearly, though it is not easily described in a word. We stumble over 'actuality', 'grip of fact', 'sense of detail', 'realism', yet with the conviction that we are proceeding in the right direction. We desire to express not merely the talent of close observation, but the power of producing, by a cumulation of touches, a quick and perfect image to the reader. What we are really thinking of is 'intimacy' of style. Scottish literature has no monopoly of this, it is to be found in the best work everywhere, and is indeed a first axiom of artistic method, no matter what processes of selection and recollection may follow; but in Scots the zest for handling a multitude of details rather than for seeking broad effects by suggestion is very persistent. . . . Everywhere it is the Dutch style — interiors, country folk and town 'bodies', farmyard and alehouse; everywhere a direct and convincing familiarity; little or nothing left out and much almost pedantically accurate."

He finds this quality not only in Burns and Scott but in the Makars, and we may accept it, therefore, as distinctively Scottish. He then goes on to say: "An exhaustive survey of all this material would show that the completed effect of the piling up of details is one of movement, suggesting the action of a concerted dance or the canter of a squadron. We have gone astray if we call this art merely meticulous, a pedant's or cataloguer's vanity in words, as some foolish persons have inclined to make charge against the 'antiquary' Scott. The whole is not always lost in the parts; it is not a compilation impressive only because it is greater than any of its contributing elements, but often single in result and, above all things, lively. For which reason our earlier epithet of 'Dutch' must be understood 'with a difference', if we incline to think only of the careful brush-work of every tile and pot-lid in an interior. The verse-forms of both popular and artificial Scots poetry aid this purpose of movement — in the stanzas of the *Cherrie and the Slae*, in *Philotus*, in some of Douglas's Prologues, in *Christis Kirk* and *Peblis to the Play*, and in much of Burns." No description could catch more exactly the feeling and movement of the Scots poetry of observation.

But Gregory Smith continues, "the Scottish muse has . . . another mood. Though she has loved reality, sometimes to maudlin affection for the commonplace, she has loved not less the airier pleasures to be found in the confusion of the senses, in the fun of things thrown topsy-turvy, in the horns of elfland and the voices of the mountains. It is a strange union of opposites, alien as Hotspur and Glendower; not to be explained as if this liking for 'skimble-skamble stuff' were derived from the very exuberance of the poets' realism by an inevitable reaction, or were a defect of its quality, or a sort of saturnalian indulgence to the slaves of observation. The opinion, so popular with Renan's and Matthew Arnold's generation, that this whimsical delight is a Celtic heritage may or may not be true, but the attempt to find a source is useful as a reminder that this characteristic is not a mere accident, or wantoning, no matter how much of its extravagance may be a direct protest against the prose of experience. It goes better with our knowledge of Scottish character and history to accept the antagonism as real and necessary. The Scot is not a quarrelsome man, but he has a fine sense of the value of provocation, and in the clash of things and words has often found a spiritual tonic. . . . There is more in the Scottish antithesis of the real and the fantastic than is to be explained by the familiar rules of rhetoric. The sudden jostling of contraries seems to preclude any relationship by literary suggestion. The one invades the other without warning. They are the 'polar twins' of the Scottish Muse."

Gregory Smith adds that "historians and critics of Scottish literature have made scant allowance, if any, for these interruptions of the plain tale of experience, even though the poets themselves have given not a few hints of surprise at their own change of mood, and have at times attempted an explanation". He instances that strange poem, *Lichtouns Dream*, where the poet explains in the last few lines all the fancies with which it is crowded as the effects of "gentill aill", and Burns's ascription of Tam o' Shanter's adventures to whisky, and the suggestion in *Wandering Willie's Tale* that Steenie "had taken ower muckle brandy to be very certain about onything". He goes on: "We are dull indeed if we do not see in this reference to the contrast and in its explanation a quizzing of those prosaic and precise persons who must have that realism which presents everything as sober fact, within an ell of their noses. The poets seem to say: 'Here is fantasy strange enough; if you, drunkard of facts, must explain it, do so in the only way open to you, or to any "auld carlin". Be satisfied, if you think it is we who are drunk. As for us, let the contrast be unexplained, and let us make merry in this clash of strange worlds and moods.' "

Here again Gregory Smith gives the very feeling of the kind of poetry he is describing. Yet his treatment of it seems to me far less satisfactory than his treatment of the homespun poetry of observation. There is definite special pleading in the words which he puts into the mouths of the Scottish poets, words indeed which express in the most extreme form the romantic, playboy conception of poetry. Again, like the poets whose attitude he is expressing, he draws no conclusions from his own generalization. He asserts that Scottish poetry is of two kinds, the poetry of observation and the poetry of fantasy; he shows these two orders of poetry invading each other "without warning", and he "lets the contrast be unexplained", quite content that Scotsmen should "make merry in this clash of strange worlds and moods". If this habit were universal in Scotland it would be an amusing country. A literature which made merry in the clash of strange worlds and moods would be as exhilarating as if it had all been written by Lewis Carroll and Edward Lear. But as the sole complement to a literature of Dutch observation it is clearly inadequate.

Or rather it would be, if it were really the sole complement to the more realistic mode of Scottish poetry. I have tried to show that it is not, and that before the disruption of Scottish literature there were other and more satisfactory modes. Dunbar is certainly one of the best fantastic poets in Scottish literature; but his fantastic poetry is merely one of a dozen kinds that he wrote, not one of two. It was thrown off by one part of his diverse mind, and in the variety of his verse it found its due value. But of Dunbar as a figure it cannot be said that he made merry in the clash of strange worlds and moods; we have only to turn to his *Lament for the Makars* to see that, or to the magnificent poem beginning:

> Done is a battell on the dragon blak.

The same thing can be said just as little of Henryson or Douglas or Alexander Scott or Montgomery. So that we have to be on our guard when we come to Gregory Smith's main conclusion. "If a formula," he says, "is to be found [for Scottish literature] it must explain this strange combination of things unlike, of things seen in an everyday world and things which, like the elf-queen herself, neither earth nor heaven will claim. This mingling, even of the most eccentric kind, is an indication to us that the Scot, in that medieval fashion which takes all things for granted, is at his ease in both 'rooms of life', and turns to fun, and even profanity, with no misgivings. For Scottish literature is more medieval in habit than criticism has suspected, and owes some part of its picturesque strength to this freedom in passing from one mood to another. It takes some people more time than they can spare to see the absolute propriety of a gargoyle's grinning at the elbow of a kneeling saint." He adds later that "we seem to find some connexion between this double mood and the easy passing in Scottish literature between the natural and the supernatural, as if in challenge to the traditional exclusiveness of certain subjects, each within its own caste".

There is so much fine observation in this passage, so many things justly said, as, for instance, about the medieval temper of Scottish literature, that one may seem ungenerous in criticizing it. Yet it would take a great deal more evidence to prove that the Scottish poet is at ease (who, indeed, is?) in "both rooms of life", if by that is meant the visible and the invisible world. Scottish writers have certainly a strong sense of the many-sidedness of life, of the poetic side of the prosaic, and still more of the prosaic side of the poetic, as is shown so clearly by Burns and Scott in their juxtapositions of tragedy and comedy, of the lofty and the humorous. These juxtapositions are admirable, and they require a very fine balance of imagination. But Scottish fantastic poetry seems to me not to touch the second room of life at all; it is a pure escape, a pure holiday, whose ruling spirit is a Protestant Pope of Unreason: again we come upon the popular medieval habit of Scottish poetry. The fact that it is a poetry of escape is no reason for blaming it, but neither, on the other hand, is it a reason for taking it too seriously. To show what I mean I shall set an example of it side by side with an example of English fantastic poetry. The first is from *Ane Litill Interlud of the Droichis* (that is of the dwarfs) attributed by some to Dunbar:

> My fore-grandschir, hecht Fyn Mackcowll,
> That dang the Devil, and gart him yowl,
> The skyis rain'd when he wad scowl,
>   He troublit all the air:

He gat my gudeschir Gog Magog;
Ay, when he dansit the warld wad shog;
Ten thousand ellis yede in his frog
    Of Hieland plaidis and mair.

And yet he was of tender youth;
Bot efter he grew meikle at fouth,
Eleven mile wide mett was his mouth,
    His teeth was ten mile square.
He wald upon his tais stand
And tak the starnis doun with his hand
And set them for a gold garland
    Abuve his wifis hair.

My fader meikle Gowk McMorne
Out of his moderis wame was shorn;
For littleness she was forlorne
    Siche ane kemp to bear:
Or he of age was yearis three,
He wald step over the ocean sea;
The moon sprang never abune his knee,
    The heavens had of him fear.

The other is from the English anonymous poem, *Tom of Bedlam's Song*:

I slept not since the Conquest,
Till then I never waked,
Till the rouguish boy
    Of love where I lay
Me found and stript me naked.

The moon's my constant mistress,
And the lonely owl my marrow;
    The flaming drake
    And the night-crow make
Me music to my sorrow.

I know more than Apollo,
For oft, when he lies sleeping,
    I see the stars
    At mortal wars
And the wounded welkin weeping.

The moon embrace her shepherd,
And the queen of love her warrior,
    While the first doth horn
    The star of morn,
And the next the heavenly farrier.

With a host of furious fancies,
Whereof I am commander,
    With a burning spear
    And a horse of air
To the wilderness I wander.

Both these poems belong to fantasy, but the difference between them goes far deeper than the resemblance. The first evokes a wild, humorous possibility, which exists in no sphere, either natural or supernatural; the second creates a world. It exists in the second room of life purely; it has the completeness of a single vision, a single experience. One cannot imagine its author "explaining" it by the influence of ale or brandy, or troubling to stop and quiz "those prosaic and precise persons who must have that realism which presents everything as sober fact, within an ell of their noses", or exclaiming: "Here is fantasy strange enough. Be satisfied, if you think it is I who am drunk. As for me, let the contrast be unexplained, and let me make merry in this clash of strange worlds and moods." There is nothing self-conscious, and nothing argumentative, in the poem; to its author the experience described is just as valid as any more usual experience: he takes it seriously. He acknowledges, that is to say, the reality of the other world. Gregory Smith sees in Scottish fantastic poetry a proof that Scotsmen are at ease in both rooms of life; but the place they actually reach through this kind of poetry is a sort of half-way-house between the two. Franz Kafka in one of his aphorisms pictures a man as fastened by one collar to the earth, so that when he tries to fly too high he is pulled back again, and fastened by another to Heaven, so that when he sinks too low he is brought up in the opposite direction. Scottish fantastic poetry represents a mean altitude in which a man finds the maximum ease from these two predicaments. It is a spirited recoil from the earthly which does not take one into too inconvenient proximity to the heavenly; both collars lie easy round the poet's neck, and for the time being he can imagine, if he pleases, that there is no collar at all. Finally the drag of ordinary gravity pulls him back to earth again, and to explanations which will satisfy the ordinary man: drink being the most natural of these. *Tam o' Shanter* belongs to this kind of poetry, for drink is its principle as well as its imaginative explanation.

Kings may be blest, but Tam was glorious,
O'er a' the ills o' life victorious.

Wordsworth was so struck by the second of these lines that he discovered a philosophy in it, and indeed it is the true philosophy of this kind of poetry. The poet is victorious over all the ills of life through an imaginative intoxication which frees him from the pressure of life. But it is a temporary victory which cancels itself out with the cessation of drunkenness and the causes of drunkenness, leaving life what it was before, an inexorable shape to whom an explanation is due. Dunbar's *Dance of the Seven Deidly Sinnis* is of the same kind; it represents a double recoil from two worlds of reality such as can be got by drunkenness, a double escape through wild humour from the horrible idea of Hell and the discomfort of this world. This kind of poetry is a flying off the handle, an attempt to disconnect oneself from all worlds; an expression of pure dissociation; the formulation also, perhaps, of a wish that reality were different, both sensual reality and supersensual reality; and a flouting of things in general, of Heaven and Earth and Hell, of God and Man, of the universal frame itself. It is essentially belittling, acridly belittling in Dunbar, and genially, almost affectionately belitting in Burns. It is seen at its sourest in *The Dance of the Seven Deidly Sinnis*:

Then cried Mahoun for a Hieland padyane;
Syne ran a fiend to fetch MacFadzen,
Far northward in a neuk;

Be he the coronach had done shout,
Ersemen so gadderit him about,
In Hell great room they tuk.
Thae termagantis, with tag and tatter,
Full loud in Erse begouth to clatter,
And roup like raven and rook;
The Devil sa deavit was with their yell,
That in the deepest pot of hell
He smoorit them with smoke.

It is almost tender in Burns's *Address to the Deil*:

Lang syne in Eden's bonie yaird,
When youthfu' lovers first were pair'd,
An' all the soul of love they shar'd,
    The raptur'd hour,
Sweet on the fragrant flow'ry swaird,
    In shady bower;

Then you, ye auld, snick-drawing dog!
Ye cam to Paradise incog,
An' play'd on man a cursed brogue
    (Black be your fa!),
An' gied the infant warld a shog,
    'Maist ruin'd a'.

In these wonderful verses this belittling fantasy transcends itself for a moment; there is true pathos in the contrast, a genuine sense of both rooms of life. But that is momentary, a passing flash of Burns's genius, for the poem immediately goes on:

D'ye mind that day when in a bizz
Wi' reekit duds, an' reestit gizz,
Ye did present your smoutie phiz
'Mang better folk,
An' sklented on the man of Uzz
Your spiteful joke?

That verse too shows genius; and the kind of poetry to which it belongs is admirable as giving a flavour to a literature. But, ever since Gregory Smith's famous generalization, this quality has been accorded an exaggerated importance; it has been exalted as a major attribute of Scottish poetry, instead of an occasional mood, a periodic holiday of the imagination. As a holiday it is above all things enjoyable; but as an antithesis to prosaic experience it is inadequate, for it consists either in a comic propitiation of terrible things, as in the two poems just quoted, or in a tangential escape from the ordinary world. It does not ask for the voluntary suspension of disbelief which we bring to *Kubla Khan*. Indeed it does not ask for belief at all, for it is completely sceptical of itself. In it we find the imagination pulling one way and the intellect the other so that neither can reach its end, and finally coming to rest in the half-way house I mentioned before. I think it is not extravagant to see in this kind of poetry the ideal expression of the dichotomy which has been Scotland's ruin both in politics and in literature; not a salutary and creative factor, as is sometimes assumed, but an expression, fantastic, humorous and sometimes delightful, of a stationary disharmony, a standing frustration. For imagination and intellect do not reach a reconciliation in this poetry, but a comic deadlock. The result is not creation, but distortion. To exalt this kind of fantasy, therefore, as a major attribute of Scottish poetry, is dangerous flattery.

There is one sphere of Scottish poetry in which a sense of the other world is expressed with unconditional force: the Ballads. Compare the kind of thwarted fantasy of which I have been speaking with the best passages in the Ballads, and what does it come to? Compare it with *The Daemon Lover*:

> And aye as she turn'd her round about,
> Aye taller he seem'd to be;
> Until that the tops o' that gallant ship
> Nae taller were than he.

Or with *The Wife of Usher's Well*:

> It fell about the Martinmas,
> When nights were lang and mirk,
> The carline wife's three sons came hame,
> And their hats were o' the birk.
>
> It neither grew in syke nor ditch,
> Nor yet in ony sheugh;
> But at the gates o' Paradise
> That birk grew fair eneugh.

Or with *Thomas the Rhymer*:

> O they rade on, and farther on,
> And they waded rivers abune the knee;
> And they saw neither sun nor moon,
> But they heard the roaring of the sea.

The Scots had once this other-world vision as strongly and purely as any people; but it has disappeared; Burns had none of it; Scott had flashes of it, and Scott was the last. One has only to set it beside the Scottish poetry of fantasy to see imagination moving in freedom, and imagination chained. The difference between ballad poetry and the fantastic poetry of Scotland is that the first accepts experience, and that the second flies away from it. The second gives superficially, therefore, a greater feeling of freedom, but the first moves on the plane of freedom itself.

I should not have devoted so much space to this fantastic poetry, if it were not that Gregory Smith's generalization attributed such importance to it, and that Scottish criticism has ever since tended extravagantly to overestimate it. Gregory Smith found in this vein of fantasy the compensating quality which offset what he called the Scottish "maudlin affection for the commonplace", which we may regard as an expression of Scottish materialism. He had an uneasy feeling that the Scots are a materialistic people, as all intelligent Scotsmen must have; and he wished to prove that they are not so materialistic as they seem, indeed that they are absurdly impractical and irresponsible, gay and illogical flouters of the material world. He acknowledged, on the other hand, that they often returned to that world after these excursions and explained their behaviour in terms perfectly acceptable to it; but he did not draw the obvious conclusion from this fact. A hundred years ago Heine saw that sentimentality was the other face of materialism; but materialism has many faces. Scottish fantastic poetry is the natural recoil from a "maudlin affection for the commonplace", but it has no peculiar virtue beyond its naturalness. It is not a genuine complement to Scottish homespun poetry, completing and fulfilling it, but merely a temporary reaction bringing us back to the point where we started. To romanticize this reaction, to picture the Scotsman as making merry in a clash of strange worlds and moods (but contriving presumably to earn a living meantime) is mere sentimentality, and perpetuates an ancestral weakness of Scotland, the weakness which turned all its history into legend, mainly tawdry, and created such ludicrous misunderstandings as the myth of Bonnie Prince Charlie. The response of the Makars and the Balladists to experience was a whole response; the response of fantastic poetry is a joke followed by an explanation.

6. SUMMARY

I asked at the beginning of this essay whether Scotland had a literature, and in what sense it could be called a literature. After this brief survey it should be possible to answer this question in a rough-and-ready way. For some time, more or less corresponding to the reign of James IV, Scotland had a major poetry, written in a homogeneous language in which the poet both felt and thought naturally. That poetry never found its fulfilment in poetic tragedy, and for that and other reasons, some of them political, dwindled later into a sort of simple one-dimensional folk poetry. The disintegration of Scottish poetry was accompanied by a disintegration of the Scots language, and both calamities, again, were brought about in part by political causes. Once the language was broken up, the old fusion between thought and feeling was lost, and a far-reaching dissociation set in, one of the most characteristic expressions of which was fantasy, which was an abortive and never quite serious attempt to achieve a synthesis between thought and feeling. This is roughly the stage which Scots poetry has reached today.

For a short period towards the end of the fifteenth and the beginning of the sixteenth century, then, Scotland had the germ of a literature which with good fortune might have developed into a full and complete literature with a language of its own. How far history, and how far the

Scottish character, were responsible for the cessation of that development, it is impossible now to say. But it is clear that Scottish literature lacks whole areas which we find in others. I have already spoken of the absence of poetic drama. But Scots is also without a prose, that is a separate vehicle for thought. We cannot doubt that if its development had continued it would have had such a prose. There are a few scraps of Scots prose extant, mainly belonging to the sixteenth century, but, as Gregory Smith says, it is "unconscious of any artistic purpose as hinted at by the first southern writers from Pecocke to Fisher, and without a single touch of the craftsmanship of Malory, or even of Caxton. There is nothing in Scots then, or indeed later, like that passage of the throwing of Excalibur into the lake, or a hundred others, as good or less good, in the *Morte d'Arthur*; no confession like that of our first printer's delight in French prose, because it was 'so well and compendiously set and written', and of his ambition to make his English as fair." Yet Henryson, Douglas and Dunbar obviously thought in Scots, and had he cared the last-named would have been a brilliant critic of poetry. However we may explain it, the fact remains that there is no Scottish prose, nothing in Scots vernacular literature to call up any image of the various worlds that occur to one's mind when one mentions Montaigne, Pascal, Sir Thomas Browne, Voltaire, Rousseau, Swift, Hegel, Schopenhauer, De Quincey, Newman, and a hundred other writers. In the whole world of discourse Scots literature is a blank.

In poetry itself, apart from its great period, Scotland

has little more than two forms to show: the lyric and the ballad. Burns, Fergusson and Hogg overstepped these narrow confines, and Hugh MacDiarmid has done so in our own time. Nevertheless these two forms have been the almost unvarying staple of Scottish poetry since the sixteenth century, while England has produced a variety of poetic forms to indicate which one has only to mention the names of some of its chief poets: Spenser, Shakespeare, Donne, Milton, Pope, Blake, Wordsworth, Browning. In these the English tradition lives, and lives in perpetual change. Can we say, then, that Scottish poetry provides a satisfactory tradition for a native poet, when we consider that after its first brilliant flowering it has remained stationary, and equally barren in variety and development? I asked this question also at the beginning, but before attempting to answer it I shall have to deal first with the problem of Walter Scott.

II
SCOTT AND SCOTLAND

The main facts about Scott's life are well known, and it is unnecessary here, as well as foreign to the purpose of this book, to enter exhaustively into them. But as my aim is to show briefly how Scotland affected Scott, stimulating his imagination and at the same time conditioning it, some of these facts are relevant.

Scott was born in 1771, in Edinburgh, and was the son of a highly respectable and strict-living lawyer. Through his forbears he was connected with a number of famous Border families. "He was linked collaterally," says Lord Tweedsmuir in his biography, "through the Buccleuchs with the greater *noblesse*. He had behind him the most historic of the Border stocks in Scott and Murray and Rutherford and Swinton. He had Celtic blood from MacDougal and Campbell. Of the many painted shields on the ceiling of the hall at Abbotsford which enshrine his pedigree, only three lack a verified heraldic cognizance. Among his forbears were saints and sinners, scholars and sportsmen and men-at-arms, barons and sheep-farmers, divines and doctors of medicine, Whigs and Jacobites, Cavaliers and Quakers. Above all he had that kindest bequest of the good fairies at his cradle, a tradition, bone of his bone, of ancient pastoral, or a free life lived among clear waters and green hills as in the innocency of the world."

Scott's father was a strict, formal, ascetic, Calvinistic, but kindly and honourable man. His mother was vivacious and affectionate, with a very good memory which her son was to inherit from her, and a head stored "with ballads and proverbs and tales". It was she who introduced him to poetry, and he was a very precocious child, as is shown in a delightful letter of Mrs Cockburn's:

> "He was reading a poem to his mother when I went in. I made him read on; it was the description of a shipwreck. His passion rose with the storm. 'There's the mast gone,' says he. 'Crash it goes! They will all perish!' After his agitation he turns to me. 'That is too melancholy,' says he. 'I had better read you something more amusing.' I proposed a little chat and asked his opinion of Milton and other books he was reading, which he gave me wonderfully. One of his observations was, 'How strange it is that Adam, just new come into the world, should know everything — that must be the poet's fancy,' says he. But when he was told that he was created perfect by God, he instantly yielded. When taken to bed last night he told his aunt he liked that lady. 'What lady?' says she. 'Why, Mrs Cockburn, for I think she is a virtuoso, like myself.' 'Dear Walter,' says Aunt Jenny, 'what is a virtuoso?' 'Don't you know? Why, it's one that wishes and will know everything.' "

The boy was not quite six at the time.

Scott was a strong child, but when he was eighteen months old he had a teething fever during which he lost the use of his right leg, and as the ordinary medical treatment did no good the doctor advised that he should be sent to his grandfather's farm of Sandy Knowe in Tweeddale. Here, in his ancestral Border country, he received his first impressions of the world. The life on the farm was simple and democratic. The ewe-milkers carried him about with them, and the cow-bailie, Sandy Ormiston, became his special friend. His grandmother had a large store of wild tales of the Borders. After a brief interlude in Bath, where he was taken in the hope that it might cure his lameness, and where he saw *As You Like It*, which made a deep impression on his imagination, he returned to Sandy Knowe again to stay for almost two years.

At eight he went to Edinburgh and began his schooling. His solitary childhood had unfitted him for the society of his rough-and-tumble brothers; but he soon displayed pugnacity, though at a great cost to his feelings, for he wrote later that "such was the agony that I had internally experienced, that I have guarded against nothing more in the education of my own family, than against their acquiring habits of self-willed caprice and domination". On account of his lameness he fought his battles with other boys by an agreement that both combatants should be strapped to a deal board. When he was in his 'teens a friend of his testified that nobody was quicker to enter a fight or less inclined to leave it. At that time he was of unusual strength, and Hogg, the poet, declared of him years later that he had never met a stronger man. The delight in fighting which we find in Scott's novels was therefore a personal taste and not a mere compensation for lack of ability. His brawls were naturally less serious than those of the characters whom he created later; they were fought with cudgels and fists, not with swords and pistols. We may put them down mainly to high spirits, but they were probably animated, too, by romantic stories of Border forays, heard from the lips of his grandmother, and by an understandable resolution to prove that he was as good as his neighbour, in spite of his bad leg. It seems a reasonable hypothesis that had he not been lame he would not have fought so much as he seems to have done as a young man, and also that he might not later on have crammed his novels so full of quarrels described in a romantic vein which was quite foreign, for instance, to Fielding.

After a few years' schooling Scott was taken into his father's office, at fourteen, as an apprentice. There for over two years he was tied down to hard and uninteresting drudgery, in which Lord Tweedsmuir sees "an invaluable training for his later feats of scribing". But how deep a mark it left on him may be guessed from another observation in Lord Tweedsmuir's book: "Till the end of his life he continued to finish off a page with a flourish of the pen, and at Abbotsford used to be heard to mutter, 'There goes the old shop again'." By that time the keenness of his original exasperation must have been considerably blunted, but that inevitable flourish of the pen and that exclamation show us clearly enough how much Scott must have suffered during those years. We can guess it too from his portrait of his father in *Redgauntlet*, a portrait which still rouses in the reader quite a keen feeling of irritation, in spite of its tolerance.

At seventeen it was definitely decided that Scott should follow the law, and he was sent to the law classes at the college. He worked hard for the next three years and passed his final trials in 1792. Lord Tweedsmuir draws a portrait of him at this time: "Scott had passed into manhood with a remarkable assortment of knowledge, for from the age of five his mind had never been idle. He was a sound lawyer, especially well versed in feudal niceties. Philosophy he had never touched; nor theology, except what he had picked up from his Calvinistic tutor. In history he was widely and curiously read, and his memory for detail enabled him to retain every fragment of out-of-the-way learning which had colour and drama. He had browsed over the whole field of English literature, and was a mine of Shakespearean lore. He had enough French, German, Spanish and Italian to read the works in these languages which appealed to him; French he spoke after a fashion, but, as one of the attendants of the exiled Charles X said, it was the French of the good Sire de Joinville. He was still in the acquisitive rather than the critical stage of mental development, and his taste in poetry was for things like the lisping iambics of Mickle's *Cumnor Hall.*"

His legal career "enlarged his knowledge of the human comedy, and took him into odd by-paths", Lord Tweedsmuir says. But "he learned more from his practice than the humours of humanity, for Scots law was one of the main educative influences in his life. Its complexity and exactness formed a valuable corrective to a riotous imagination. It was the one form of science which he ever cultivated." This superposition of a complex and exact body of knowledge upon a riotous imagination is important for the understanding of Scott's work, for it is to be seen in his novels in those juxtapositions of the romantic and the prosaic which form so much of their humour, and supply so much of their pinchbeck. It was a superposition, not a reconciliation such as might have been found in a whole body of experience radiating from a centre in an autonomous society.

The conflict between Scott's imagination and experience was intensified by an event which happened before he was twenty. He fell in love with a girl of fifteen, Williamina, daughter of Sir John Stuart-Belsches of Fettercairn. She was above him in station, and his father felt obliged to inform Sir John of the attachment between the young pair. Sir John raised no obstacle, however; the friendship continued over several years, and there seems no doubt that on Scott's side it deepened into love. Sometime during 1795 he proposed to the girl, but by the end of the year he still doubted whether he was accepted. Late next year he knew definitely that his hopes were mistaken, and in 1797 Williamina married another man.

That this was a decisive event in Scott's life is clearly proved, I think, by Lord Tweedsmuir. I shall quote from him again, for nobody has put the case better. "He had cut Williamina's name on the turf of the castle gate at St

Andrews as a young lover, and thirty-four years after sat on an adjacent gravestone and wondered why the name 'should still agitate my heart'. Three months later he met Lady Jane [Williamina's mother] in Edinburgh; she was then well over seventy, and her daughter had been dead for seventeen years. The meeting was like opening a sepulchre.

" 'I fairly softened myself, like an old fool, with recalling stories, till I was fit for nothing but shedding tears and repeating verses for the whole night. This is sad work. The very grave gives up its dead, and time rolls back thirty years to add to my perplexities.'

"The emotion must have been deep which could leave such traces. He put it behind him, as he put all things of whose futility he was convinced, but it survived in the secret places of his soul. . . . He never saw Williamina again, and he did not wish to; there was no bitterness in his memory of her, but there was regret — regret perhaps less for a thing of flesh and blood than for the 'glory and the freshness of a dream'. Somewhere at the back of his mind the thought of her dwelt, and on the eve of any great misfortune she came to him in sleep. It is a strange tale, but one which carries the key to most of his life, for we shall not understand Scott unless we realize how much he lived in a secret world of his own, an inner world of dream and memory, from which he brought great treasures, but which now and then, to his undoing, invaded the world of facts."

This is a just and sensitive analysis, completely convincing except, perhaps, for the assumption that

Scott's regret was "less for a thing of flesh and blood than for the 'glory and the freshness of a dream'", for one feels that only a deep, compulsive and *physical* passion could have made Williamina appear to Scott in sleep on the eve of great misfortunes. The fact that a few months later Scott's heart was "handsomely pierced", as he himself put it, by Charlotte Carpenter, and that he married her before the year was out, only strengthens this supposition. "Scott was in wild spirits," says Lord Tweedsmuir, "during his engagement, and he raved about the lady to his friends, but it seems certain that his heart was not greatly affected." Lord Tweedsmuir goes on to say that Scott "liked the idea of marriage as a step in that progress in life to which one side of him (his father's side) was vowed". But if Scott's attachment to Williamina was indeed a deep and passionate one, and his disappointment so extreme that some of his friends dreaded the consequences, there is clearly another interpretation for his marriage and the haste with which he rushed into it, and that can be found in his own words twelve years later, quoted by Lord Tweedsmuir: "Folk who have been nearly drowned in bathing rarely . . . venture . . . a second time out of their depth." His wife, his biographer adds, "never entered into his secret world".

Lord Tweedsmuir says of Scott's love for Williamina that "he put it behind him, as he put all things of whose futility he was convinced". To say that that passion was futile is to pass a practical judgment upon it, and I think that Lord Tweedsmuir is probably right in assuming that this is what Scott did; he could not marry Williamina, and therefore the less he thought of her the better. But the passion "survived in the secret places of his soul". His response to it, that is to say, was in one sense inadequate; and I think it may be reasonably explained by the superposition of a relatively narrow kind of judgment upon a world of experience greater than it, a superposition similar to that of the complex and exact body of Scottish law upon a riotous imagination. Scotland was not an organic society with its own conventions of thought and sensibility; except in the ordinary commerce of daily life, it was trying to imitate England; and in matters of feeling it was inclined in its uncertainty to come down plump on the side of plain practical judgment. I do not want to lay too much importance on such conventions; there are certain situations in which they are clearly of very little help. Nevertheless Scott lived in a Calvinistic country which had little respect for the more human passions, and though he was not himself tinged with Calvinistic ways of thought, he had been indoctrinated with the complex and exact creed of Scots law, which was just as impervious to these passions as Calvinism had been. I do not want to labour this point, and shall be content if I can show that the discipline of Scots law was not an adequate complement to Scott's riotous imagination and violent feelings, that something else was required, and that the Scotland of his time could not supply it.

Scott, then, put his disastrous love affair behind him. Lord Tweedsmuir praises him for this, and compares him favourably with the poets "who wear their hearts on their sleeves and protest to the world that the pang of an hour is an eternal sorrow. Scott's passion was a profounder emotion than any which the lives of Burns or Shelley or Byron can show." This may be true, but the question is not whether his passion was profounder, but whether he did better in burying it than in acknowledging it. Did he do better than Shakespeare in his Sonnets, or than Keats in his letters? This is not a rhetorical question; we can never tell whether, given his nature and the circumstances, Scott acted rightly or wrongly; but to acknowledge a passion within oneself is at least to take it seriously, and a man of imagination who does so will be able to treat passion seriously in his works. Shakespeare did so, and Keats, had he lived, would no doubt have done so. Scott never succeeded in this respect except, imperfectly, in *The Bride of Lammermoor*, a book which he wrote in a delirium of pain, so that "he had no recollection of its composition, and pronounced it, after his first anxious reading, to be 'monstrous, gross and grotesque'". It is doubtful, I think, whether Scott would have put his unsuccessful love affair behind him so summarily if he had belonged to a different country. It may be objected that Wordsworth did exactly the same thing at about the same time; but Wordsworth was a solitary, always disinclined to unbosom himself, and Scott was in most things open and frank. It is not unreasonable, then, to refer Scott's failure in the imaginative treatment of passion to the way in which he dealt with his own passion for Williamina Stuart, and that, again, to the fact that he lived in an imperfectly integrated society where many aspects of life were ignored, and sensibility was an imported product.

Scott's advance in the law was rapid, and he was soon earning a handsome income. Of this aspect of his life I intend to say nothing, nor of the series of financial blunders by which he finally found himself, with the failure of Constable, involved in such a maze of debt. When Lord Tweedsmuir writes of the "inner world of dream and memory" into which Scott retreated after his disastrous love affair, and says that, while he brought "great treasures" from it, it also "now and then to his undoing invaded the world of facts", he no doubt means Scott's complicated dealings with the Ballantyne brothers and George Constable. No one, I think, would say that any serious moral blame attaches to Scott because of these dealings; and all the world knows of the heroic fight by which he tried to extricate himself honourably from their consequences.

Scott's first important work was the *Minstrelsy of the Scottish Border*. This book was essentially an attempt to save something of a Scotland that was disappearing. "By such efforts," Scott said, "feeble as they are, I may contribute something to the history of my native country; the peculiar features of whose manners and character are daily melting and dissolving into those of her sister and ally. And, trivial as may appear such an offering to the Manes of a kingdom, once proud and independent, I hang it upon her altar with a mixture of feelings which I shall not attempt to describe."

There is no mistaking the emotion in these words, and I think it is not hard to guess at the mixture of feelings which Scott shrank from describing. He was a man to whom the established order was sacred. The Union between Scotland and England was an accomplished fact, a solid part of the established order. He accepted it as such, and although Jacobite sentiment still excited his imagination, it had no effect on his practical judgment. Yet temperamentally he was sympathetic towards Jacobitism as a revolt against the old by the still more old, the only kind of revolt that he could countenance. But "his mind was in a high degree concrete and practical," says Lord Tweedsmuir; "he might take arms against a proven abuse but not against a dubious theory, and his devotion to the past made him abhor all that was speculative and rootless. . . . He was a Tory, not on the philosophical grounds of Burke and Bolingbroke, but because as a poet he loved the old ways, and as a practical man would conserve them, however logically indefensible, so long as they seemed to serve their purpose. So he joined heartily in breaking the heads of Irish students who sang rebel songs in the theatre, and, when the volunteering movement began, wrote to Kelso for 'a strong gelding such as would suit a stalwart dragoon', to purchase which he was prepared to sell his collection of Scottish coins." This was at the time of the French Revolution, which seemed to him, in Lord Tweedsmuir's words, "a carnival of disorder distasteful to the lawyer, and a menace to his country hateful to the patriot". The "country" was Great Britain, not Scotland; there was no doubt of Scott's allegiance to that and the Hanoverian House.

At the same time he saw "the peculiar features of

[Scotland's] manners and character . . . daily melting and dissolving into those of her sister and ally". His strong instinct for continuity showed him Scotland as "a kingdom, once proud and independent". It is clear from this passage that Scott regarded with acute concern the inevitable melting and dissolving of Scotland's manners and character into those of England, and that he looked back upon Scotland's lost kingdom, "once proud and independent", with a still keener emotion. In the novels which he wrote later he romanticized that loss, and his very adherence to the established order made it inevitable that he should do so, for his allegiance was divided. But the feeling in this passage is a feeling of urgent unease and apprehension, somewhat akin to Mr Yeats's

> Things fall apart; the centre cannot hold,

and Mr Eliot's

> These fragments I have shored against my ruins.

One has the impression already that Scott can find a real image of Scotland only in the past, and knows that the nation which should have formed both his theme and his living environment as a writer is irremediably melting away around him. He was nearer the beginning of that process than we are, he saw its end more clearly, and had a more complete image of what was involved.

But he "loved the old ways". We know that quite early, when he was still a child, he began to collect mementoes of the past. His taste was peculiarly retentive, like his memory. His first few years spent at Sandy Knowe explain Abbotsford, as Lord Tweedsmuir finely points out. "He won, too," Lord Tweedsmuir goes on, "an insight — the unconscious but penetrating insight of a child — into a society which was fast disappearing, the society from which the Ballads had sprung. A whole lost world had been reborn in his brain, and the learning of after-years was only to supplement the far more potent imaginative construction of childhood." The *Minstrelsy*, then, may be regarded as a preliminary attempt to gather the scattered limbs of a Scotland which even in his childhood had been falling asunder. His first long poem was *The Lay of the Last Minstrel*; the emphasis is once more on something dead and gone. This strong instinctive reaching back into the past may therefore have been an unconscious attempt by Scott to win a complete theme on which to write and a complete order within which to write, in a present which was melting and dissolving away. By his collection of all sorts of relics and mementoes of Scotland's history — it began early and continued till his death — he conserved concretely a broken image of the lost kingdom. A broken image, and, it may have occurred to him at times, a somewhat absurd one. "What a life mine has been!" he wrote towards the end, "half-educated, almost wholly neglected or left to myself, stuffing my head with the most nonsensical trash." And his rooms too.

This judgment of Scott on his own life, this epitaph on his own work, is not only moving, but throws a great deal of light on his predicament as a Scottish writer. What did he mean by saying that he was almost wholly neglected or left to himself? He could not have been thinking of his early education, for his mother introduced him to literature at an age when few children have discovered it, and his sickly childhood assured him more attention than most children receive. By a fortunate chance that attention was extremely suitable to him, awakening and stimulating his imagination. As a youth and a young man he associated with people of intelligence in a city which prided itself on its intelligence. After he became famous he certainly never suffered from neglect. Yet we cannot doubt his sincerity in saying that he had been almost wholly left to himself; and all one can think is that in these words he expressed a sense of something lacking in the whole life of his country: that binding and directing power which would have given unity and meaning to his work. His mother's influence, his early illnesses, his friendships as a boy and a young man had all been favourable to the development of his genius; yet, in spite of these, his strongest feeling was that he had somehow been left to himself. I said at the beginning of this essay that Scott wrote in a sort of vacuum, and I cannot help feeling that what he expressed in these words was a consciousness of that fact, not disappointment with his friends, but rather a sense of a general blank except for them. "He had mingled intimately," says Lord Tweedsmuir, "with every class and condition of men; he had enough education to broaden his outlook and not enough to dim it; he was familiar alike with city and moorland, with the sown and the desert, and he escaped the pedantry of both the classroom and the drawing-room." But this life which he knew so comprehensively had no centre, no heart radiating a living influence which would have made it impossible for him to feel neglected. The "most nonsensical trash" was the scattered fragments of Scotland's past which he brooded over in his mind while he watched the Scottish tradition vanishing. It was "nonsensical trash" because there was hardly anything in Scotland's present to correspond to it, and nothing at all which could replace it; for though it might seem trash, it had a centre; it formed an organic whole, and the new Scotland did not.

I have stopped over these two intimate utterances of Scott because they seem to me to illumine his novels. He was by instinct a Conservative who believed in the established order and tradition. But the phase which Scotland had reached in his time involved him in a divided allegiance. The established order was the Union, and possessing, as he did, "a mind in a high degree concrete and practical", prepared "to take arms against a proven abuse but not against a dubious theory", he had no choice but to adhere to it; for it was rooted in history and sanctified by the past. But at the same time he saw this established order gradually destroying another established order, that of Scotland. That order was equally old, equally rooted in history and sanctified by the past, and moreover it was the order to which he was most intimately bound by birth, early memory and the compulsion of his imagination. From this inward conflict he never escaped. It is the underlying theme of his three greatest novels, *Old Mortality, The Heart of Midlothian*, and *Redgauntlet*; and it is deeply entangled with all his stories of Scottish life except the more purely contemporary and local ones such as *Guy Mannering*. We find it in his two romances about Mary Stuart; it recurs in *Waverley* and again in *Rob Roy*. In all these novels, directly or indirectly, Scott is working out his conflicting allegiances to Scotland and England. But as that conflict was a thing of the past, and its solution had already been reached in the established order of the Union, his treatment of it was inevitably a little romantic in the bad sense; the main figure, the hero, is never seriously involved in the calamities of his country; the actual theme may be a national disaster, but to him it becomes as harmless as an escapade: an excuse, at most, for a set of exciting adventures, crammed with fights and escapes. Henry Morton in *Old Mortality* is the only one of Scott's heroes who is deeply implicated in the political events of the story. His final escape from the consequences of his share in them is plausible enough; but the same cannot be said of Scott's other young heroes.

At his most serious, then, Scott is concerned with this conflict of allegiances. *Old Mortality* contains his most penetrating criticism of Scottish life, and the theme is more definitely Scottish than that of any other of his major novels. But the climax of the action is resolved by English interposition, that is by the appearance of the English soldiery at Bothwell Brig. There Scott shows alien unity and strength arrayed against native dissension and weakness, and in its essentials the picture might have served equally well for Scotland's state at the Union, or for the state of Scott's own mind. It kindled his imagination immediately and produced one of Henry Morton's best speeches. Morton had just returned from his interview with Monmouth, and he addressed the disunited Covenanters in these words:

> "I bring from the enemy an offer to treat, if you incline to lay down your arms. I can assure you the means of making an honourable defence, if you are of more manly tempers. The time flies fast on. Let us resolve either for peace or war; and let it not be said of us in future days, that six thousand Scottish men in arms had neither courage to stand their ground and fight it out, nor prudence to treat for peace, nor even the coward's wisdom to retreat in good time and with safety. What signifies quarrelling on points of church-discipline, when the whole edifice is threatened with total destruction? O remember, my brethren, that the last and worst evil which God brought upon the people whom he had once chosen — the last and worst punishment of their blindness and hardness of heart, was the bloody dissensions which rent asunder their city, even when the enemy were thundering at their gates!"

In this speech Scott is fighting out a past battle of Scotland and describing what he would have done or what he would have liked to do, had he lived in the seventeenth century instead of writing in the nineteenth. His conflict of allegiances finds in such passages a sort of *post-mortem* resolution; he takes in imagination a step which history has made impossible. *Old Mortality* is his grimmest novel, and also the one in which he shows the greatest genius for political delineation. It is consequently his best criticism of Scottish history and Scottish character.

In *The Heart of Midlothian* the confrontation of Scottish and English interests is more urbane; the melting and dissolving of Scottish ways into English has proceeded much further, for we have passed from the seventeenth century to the eighteenth; and the outcome of the action is not a national defeat, but a minor triumph for Scotland over a purely personal matter. What precipitates the climax is not a conflict between the two countries, but rather an incompatibility, whose effects, however, are acutely galling to Scottish pride.

It is in *Redgauntlet* that Scott's conflict of allegiances achieves its final expression. Lord Tweedsmuir says finely that this novel "stands to Scott's greatest novels much as *Antony and Cleopatra* stands to Shakespeare's four major tragedies". This comparison is very apt, for there is in *Redgauntlet* a splendour of passion, and a sense of great forces overarching and environing the action itself, which we find in none of the other novels. In *Antony and Cleopatra* this feeling of all-embracing splendour is justified by the setting, the irresistible power of Rome, even in division; but in *Redgauntlet* it is very difficult to explain except as an expression of the intense conflict in Scott's own mind. For the theme is a minor and somewhat absurd Jacobite adventure, which has so little chance of success that the

English Government wisely decides to ignore it. Nevertheless in the leader of that adventure, Redgauntlet himself, Scott produced his one character of more than merely practical heroism. Redgauntlet seems to come more wholly out of what Lord Tweedsmuir calls Scott's "secret world" than any other character that he ever created. In the fine interview between Redgauntlet and his nephew Dairsie, one has the feeling that Scott is uttering his deepest convictions as he rarely did elsewhere. Dairsie, who is Redgauntlet's prisoner, says: "Misfortune — early deprivation — has given me the privilege of acting for myself, and constraint shall not deprive me of an Englishman's best privilege."

I quote Redgauntlet's reply:

> "The true cant of the day," said Redgauntlet, in a tone of scorn. "The privilege of free action belongs to no mortal — we are tied down by the fetters of duty — our mortal path is limited by the regulations of honour — our most indifferent actions are but meshes of the web of destiny by which we are all surrounded. . . .
>
> "The liberty of which the Englishman boasts gives as little real freedom to its owner as the despotism of an eastern Sultan permits to his slave. The usurper, William of Nassau, went forth to hunt, and thought, doubtless, that it was an act of his own royal pleasure that the horse of his murdered victim was prepared for his kingly sport. But Heaven had other views, and before the sun was high a stumble of that very animal over an obstacle so inconsider-

> able as a mole-hillock cost the haughty rider his life and his usurped crown. Do you think an inclination of the rein could have avoided that trifling impediment? I tell you it crossed his way as inevitably as all the long chain of the Caucasus could have done. Yes, young man, in doing and suffering we play but the part allotted by Destiny, the manager of this strange drama — stand bound to act no more than is prescribed, to say no more than is set down for us; and yet we mouth about free-will, and freedom of thought and action, as if Richard must not die, or Richmond conquer, exactly where the Author has decreed it shall be so!"

The man who wrote that was the same man who wrote Lucy's song in *The Bride of Lammermoor*:

> Look not thou on beauty's charming,
> Sit thou still when kings are arming,
> Taste not when the wine-cup glistens,
> Speak not when the people listens.
> Stop thine ear against the singer,
> From the red gold keep thy finger,—
> Vacant heart, and hand and eye,
> Easy live and quiet die.

But the sense of the vanity of effort, the illusoriness of freedom, does not lead Redgauntlet to a life of resignation, but to one of violent action. He is a hero in Nietzsche's definition: that is, a man to whom success and failure are merely responses. He seems to incarnate, against his will,

Scott's conviction that Scotland was bound to lose its nationality, and that Scottish manners and character must unavoidably melt and dissolve into those of England: that, in the striking phrase about William of Nassau, this fate lay in Scotland's path "as inevitably as all the long chain of the Caucasus could have done". Yet in spite of it Redgauntlet continues the fight, "tied down by the fetters of duty", "limited by the regulations of honour". This fated conflict against fate reaches its resolution in a passage unique in the Waverley Novels: the finest passage in the heroic style that Scott ever wrote. The little band of Jacobites are waiting to come to a decision in an inn beside the Solway. Everything seems already lost, for the Prince and his followers cannot agree at the last moment. Then news arrives that a party of English soldiers are approaching, and General Campbell, their commander, presently enters. There is a short parley, and this is what follows:

> "In one word, General Campbell," said Redgauntlet, "is it to be peace or war? You are a man of honour, and we can trust you."
>
> "I thank you, sir," said the General; "and I reply that the answer to your question rests with yourself. Come, do not be fools, gentlemen. There was perhaps no great harm meant or intended by your gathering together in this obscure corner for a bear-bait or a cock-fight, or whatever other amusement you may have intended; but it was a little imprudent, considering how you stand with the government, and it has occasioned some anxiety.

Exaggerated accounts of your purpose have been laid before the government by the information of a traitor in your own counsels; and I was sent down post to take the command of a sufficient number of troops, in case these calumnies should be found to have any real foundation. I have come here, of course, sufficiently supported both with cavalry and infantry to do whatever might be necessary; but my commands are — and I am sure they agree with my inclination — to make no arrests, nay, to make no further inquiries of any kind, if this good assembly will consider their own interest, as far as to give up their immediate purpose, and return quietly home to their own houses."

"What! — all?" exclaimed Sir Richard Glendale — "all, without exception?"

"ALL, without one single exception," said the General; "such are my orders. If you accept my terms, say so, and make haste; for things may happen to interfere with his Majesty's kind purposes towards you all."

"His Majesty's kind purposes!" said the Wanderer. "Do I hear you aright, sir?"

"I speak the King's very words, from his very lips," replied the General. 'I will,' said his Majesty, 'deserve the confidence of my subjects by reposing my security in the fidelity of the millions who acknowledge my title — in the good sense and prudence of the few who continue, from the errors of education, to disown it.' His Majesty will not even believe that the most zealous Jacobites who yet remain can nourish a thought of exciting civil war, which must be fatal to their families and themselves, besides spreading bloodshed and ruin through a peaceful land. He cannot even believe of his kinsman, that he would engage brave and generous, though mistaken men, in an attempt which must ruin all who have escaped former calamities; and he is convinced that, did curiosity or any other motive lead that person to visit this country, he would soon see it was his wisest course to return to the Continent, and his Majesty compassionates his situation too much to offer any obstacle to his doing so."

"Is this real?" said Redgauntlet. "Can you mean this? Am I — are all — are any of these gentlemen at liberty, without interruption, to embark in yonder brig, which, I see, is now again approaching the shore?"

"You, sir — all — any of the gentlemen present," said the General — "all whom the vessel can contain, are at liberty to embark, uninterrupted by me; but I advise none to go off who have not powerful reasons unconnected with the present meeting, for this will be remembered against no one."

"Then, gentlemen," said Redgauntlet, clasping his hands together as the words burst from him, "the cause is lost for ever!"

That final exclamation of Redgauntlet is the supreme point which Scott touched in this kind of imagination, and his strangest utterance, if we compare it with the words of his other heroes; for they are always sanguine in their belief in the effectiveness of physical courage and physical action. Redgauntlet's spirit is very different from that of Henry Morton when he exclaims to the wavering Covenanters: "Silence your senseless clamours! Yonder is the enemy! On maintaining the bridge against him, depend our lives, as well as our hope to reclaim our laws and liberties. There shall at least one Scottish man die in their defence. Let anyone who loves his country follow me!" "Tied down by the fetters of duty", "limited by the regulations of honour", Redgauntlet would have been prepared to take the same course in a situation even more hopeless. But he is confronted by something against which all his courage becomes powerless: an act of grace which is at the same time an act of irresistible power. So his cry is one of pure loss, in which a whole world, the world of action which Scott created, breathes itself out and dies beyond resurrection. But at the same time it is the acknowledgment of another world, another order, equally great, or greater, though still only guessed at, and incapable of making itself known except in a mere isolated act: a world in which we can feel the spirit of an unknown future as clearly as we recognize in the other the spirit of the known past. Whether when Scott made Redgauntlet exclaim that "the cause is lost for ever", he meant the cause of Scotland without being conscious of it, or whether he had in mind a greater issue, an issue transcending history, it is impossible to say. Probably a variety of blind and partly buried feelings found utterance in that strange cry; and what it finally signified was no doubt that conviction of the vanity of action which came to him clean out of his secret world. Yet at the time when he wrote this scene England was overcoming Scotland and dissolving its ancient tradition of life by the same means by which the English king overcame Redgauntlet's hopes: that is by a magnanimous gesture to which there was no effective reply. The elements of the situation were there, at any rate; the conflict of allegiances within Scott's mind was also there; and in this exclamation of Redgauntlet, whatever else we may have, we have the supreme, though still two-sided and equivocal, expression of that conflict.

Scott, I have suggested, reached back into the past of Scotland to win a complete theme on which to write and a complete order within which to write. This led him to stuff his head with "the most nonsensical trash", to use his own words; the trash being trash and nonsensical because it had little reference to the Scottish life of his time, and because the events with which it dealt were already settled for good. A people who lose their nationality create a legend to take its place. The reality of a nation's history lies in its continuity, and the present is its only guarantee. English history is real to us, because England as a living organic unity is real to us; all its past is gathered up in that unity, and still exists in it. But where national unity is lost the past is lost too, for the connection between the present and the past has been broken, and the past turns therefore into legend, into the poetry of pure memory. Scott saw Scottish life melting and dissolving away, and remembered a kingdom once proud and independent: and so in a fit of impatience he could refer to the relics of that kingdom as the most nonsensical trash. He could not have done so had he been an Englishman looking back on English history, for he would have found the confirmation of that history everywhere round him.

But, Lord Tweedsmuir says, "the learning of after-years was only to supplement the far more potent imaginative construction of childhood". The materials which went into that construction were not drawn from the ancient kingdom of Scotland, which was a unity, but from the traditional life of the Borders, which was already a memory, for it came to an end at the beginning of the seventeenth century. "The Borderer," says Lord Tweedsmuir, "differed in certain ways from the rest of his countrymen. He lived in an enclave of his own, for, though on the main track of marching armies, he was a little remote from the centres of national life. His eyes did not turn north to the capital, but south to the English frontier, where danger lay, and around him to his urgent local concerns. He lived under a clan system, different from that of the Highlands, but hardly less compelling. This absorption in special interests kept the Borderer, gentle and simple, from sharing largely in those national movements which had their origin in the Scottish midlands and the eastern littoral. The wars of religion, for example, affected him little. The Border bred few noted Covenant enthusiasts, as it sent few men to Montrose's standard. It was damp tinder for the fires of either reaction or revolution.

"Yet the centuries of guerilla warfare had produced something more than hardihood and independence. The Border was the home of harpers and violers, and from it came some of the loveliest of northern airs, and most of the greatest ballads in any literature. It had always had a tradition of rude minstrelsy, for during the peace of the winter season, at the Yule and Hogmanay revels, at the burgh fairs, at sheep clippings and 'kirns', and at the shieling doors in the long summer twilights, wandering minstrels would sing of old days, of the fairies in the greenwood and the kelpies in the loch, and of some deed of prowess the rumour of which had drifted across the hills. Out of this tradition, perhaps some time in the sixteenth century, the great ballads were made by singers whose names have been lost — maybe the dead poets chronicled in Dunbar's 'Lament of the Makars'. The innominate balladists left behind them poetry which often reached the highest levels of art, and which at the same time woke an immediate response in those for whom it was composed. So the Borderer, however scanty his learning, fell heir to a body of great literature, passed by word of mouth from father to son."

So much for the Border of legend, into which Scott sank his imagination. Lord Tweedsmuir gives also a picture of Border society at the time when Scott was a child. "A village had its assorted craftsmen," he says, "which made it independent of the towns, its wauk-mill and corn-mill, its schoolmaster and its minister. The bonnet-laird farmed his own land; on the great estates there were tenants cultivating large acreages, and the lairds, since they were themselves prosperous, were as a rule good masters. The Border yeoman was a great lover of sport, an inheritance from his active forbears, and came nearer to the English type of hunting farmer than to the ordinary Scots tacksman. In the upland glens the shepherds made a community by themselves — a strong and responsible race, men of the 'lang stride and the clear eye', accustomed to take many risks in their calling, for the most part literate and for the most part pious, but living close to tradition and the elder world of fairies. The youth of Leyden and Hogg gives a picture of their lives. If superstition was always at their elbow, the spirit of critical independence was also there. They were under no blind bondage either to creed or custom. The householder would stop his reading of the Bible at family prayers with the remark: 'If it hadna been the Lord's will, that verse had been better left out.' They lived in a semi-patriarchal society, where the laird was king, but they dealt with him as free men. He was greater and richer than they, but of the same blood, for a Scott or a Kerr, whose hirsel lay at the back of beyond, could count far-away kin with Buccleuch or Lothian. The clan system still survived in a wholesome and universal pride of race. Most Borderers rightly held themselves to be gently born."

This, then, was the life which provided the materials for the imaginative construction of Scott's childhood, and determined the shape it was to take later. The first thing to be remarked of this Border society is that it was a clan society, not an ordinary civil society. This clan society survived at the time when Scott first became aware of it only "in a wholesome and universal pride of race", and no longer in its earlier militant form, from which the subject-matter and the inspiration of the Ballads sprang. These

Ballads had been handed down, however, from father to son, so that the older world still lived on in them. Up to the beginning of the seventeenth century, when the governments of Scotland and England tamed it, the Border had been the most lawless part of Scotland, and "the Borderer differed in certain ways from the rest of his countrymen". Disputes were settled in this Debatable Land by the sword, not by the law. It was a sort of no-society, for it had no centre; but it had, on the other hand, a strong tradition, and that tradition reached Scott in the form of poetic legend. Now it seems to me that this tradition drunk in by Scott as a child influenced his whole conception of society as reflected in his novels, and helps to account particularly for the part which he assigns to fighting, for his purely aesthetic delight in adventure in itself as an escape from the uninteresting limitations of ordinary life.

I am conscious that in trying to demonstrate this I shall not always have the reader's agreement, or always be able to justify my inferences. What I mean, roughly, when I say that the old Border tradition influenced Scott's conception of society is that in his chief novels he almost invariably chose an unruly period which resembled the generic state of Border society, and in ranging through history merely went on repeating again and again an image of that society. His imagination was irresistibly attracted by interregnums of civilization, by times when the normal conventions of civilized life were abrogated and it was not only a pleasure, but a permissible pleasure, for men to fight as much as they cared. On the other hand his practical sense and his strong devotion to law and order forbade him to allow his young heroes to appear on the side of sedition except by mischance or as supernumeraries: they might have all the excitement they pleased, but their views must be unimpeachable. They might come in contact with Jacobite rebels and Highland sheep-stealers, and enjoy the contact; but they must not deliberately seek it, or take rebellion seriously, even if it were the rebellion of the old against the relatively new. And finally they must escape all the more painful consequences of their involuntary participation, when at last, reluctantly perhaps, but firmly, order, the established order, is reinstated again. Many disagreeable things will have happened during the period of lawlessness; most likely a number of people will have been killed; but the hero must return to safety and order without a scar to prevent him from enjoying them. For a while, that is to say, the hero enjoys all the pleasures of lawlessness, since he exists in a sort of dateless Border country outside the law; then society, firmly but benevolently, gathers him into its arms, none the worse of his holiday, and quite certain henceforth to be a decent and orderly citizen.

Now in this arrangement of experience, so convenient and so unconvincing, it seems to me that we find again the conflict within Scott's mind which I have tried to expose in its various forms: the conflict between his riotous imagination, nourished on Border legend, and his practical sense, disciplined by Scots law; the incompatibility between his allegiance to Scotland and the past he was rooted in, and England and the rootless present, which was only another form of the same conflict. The working resolution which he achieved for this conflict in his novels consisted of this permitted indulgence in lawlessness — his concession to Scotland's claims, now become illegal — followed by the sober superposition of law — his acknowledgment of England's right and the right of the established order. This resolution was not a true one, and it was untrue for reasons I have already given: that the discipline of Scots law was not an adequate completion for a riotous imagination, and that the conflict of allegiances in Scott's mind, given the situation he found himself in, was finally insoluble. So the form his approximate solution took was the story of adventure.

What happens in the story of adventure? The characters, or at least those that engage our sympathies, break the laws of civilized life and yet as by magic escape the consequences of their actions. There is a pleasant hiatus between cause and effect, and fate behaves with benevolent irresponsibility. I have attributed Scott's love for situations of this kind to his early saturation with Border legend; but that is only a partial explanation, for it does not account for this benevolent irresponsibility of fate. A Borderer of the heroic ballad era might reckon with likelihood on evading the law, but he was not so sure of escaping the revenge of his enemies: the Ballads begin lawlessly but end tragically. The hiatus between cause and effect in Scott's novels, the imperviousness of his heroes to the consequences of their actions, cannot be explained, I think, except by the fact that he was born and brought up in a sort of vacuum, a country without a centre which could gather up within itself and give meaning to all the actions of the people who composed it. These people in Scott's time were peaceful on the whole, but the peace they enjoyed was not their own peace; civilized, but not with their own civilization; and so when they broke that peace and sinned against that civilization, the real offence easily faded into a fictitious one, with only theoretical consequences. Scott's heroes escape unscathed because they exist in a No Man's Land very like the Scotland of his day, which was civilized but without that living spirit of civilization which creates its own centre of life and goes on nourishing society from it. To offend against that civilization was therefore only a conventional transgression, unless it took the universally contemned forms of theft and murder. One has only to compare Fielding's attitude to lawlessness with Scott's to see the difference in instinctive outlook between a man living in an organic society and a man living in a sort of law-abiding limbo.

I began this inquiry by asking what Scotland did for Scott, and I have tried briefly to show what it was able to give him and what it could not give him. Nature endowed him with a genius universal in its scope. Scotland provided a body of heroic legend for that genius to work upon. But it could not give him a complete framework of living experience on which to nourish his powers and exercise them; in other words, it could not give him a basis for the profound criticism of life of which there is no doubt that he was capable, as can be seen from a few of his lyrics, drawn from his secret world, and such scenes as the climax of *Redgauntlet*. It could not give him a tradition, for its tradition was melting and dissolving away; so it offered him a legend instead. Yet his essential gift was for the delineation of contemporary life, and his work is greatest where we feel in it the shock of immediate experience. If the life he knew had had a real framework, if it had not been melting and dissolving away before him, he would have had a theme worthy of his powers, and he would have had no need to stuff his head with "the most nonsensical trash". But instead of a real framework, he had to fall back on legend, and so his novels consist, as I said before, of flesh and blood and pasteboard. He is the greatest Scotsman, but there can be little doubt that he might have been incalculably greater had his environment been a different one.

I have said nothing about Scott's relation to the Scottish vernacular, since his relation to the society or no-society in which he lived seemed to me of far more importance. But his attitude to Scots was pretty much the same as I have outlined already in the first part of this essay. Where he wished to express feelings of more than ordinary seriousness and range, or feelings modified by thought, he employed English, using Scots for the simplest purposes of humour and pathos. His Scots, it is true, was far better than his English, and he produced in his dialogue the best Scots prose that has ever been written. But as the Scots vernacular did not come out of a unity, he felt that it could not express a unity; so for the structural, the unifying, part of his work he relied upon English. This again is bound up with his divided allegiance and his final acceptance of the established order. But the determining fact was a social and political one: that he lived in a country which could not give an organic form to his genius.

III
CONCLUSIONS

I began this essay by asking certain questions touching the present state of literature in Scotland. In trying to answer these questions I found myself involved in three main lines of inquiry: into the Scots language as a vehicle for literature, into the Scottish literary tradition, and into the political and social state of Scotland. I reluctantly came to the conclusion that all three were unsatisfactory as bases for a genuinely autonomous literature.

This conclusion is negative, and an inquiry such as the present might be expected to produce a positive one. It appears to me, however, that it is the task of my readers to supply that for themselves; if they are sufficiently interested in Scottish literature; for a general evil can only be remedied by co-operative thought and co-operative will: all that any individual can offer is suggestions. So my main concern has been to describe the actual state of Scottish literature, not to show how I think it can be cured; for in doing the one I could expect some measure of agreement, and in doing the other I could expect none. The first thing needful is obviously to see the position as it is.

Yet no Scottish writer can regard the present state of Scottish literature without sorrow or exasperation, and a wish to do something about it. I shall therefore describe the direction in which I think it should develop; but I cannot expect general agreement with my suggestions, and I claim no particular consideration for them.

First, as to the language of Scottish literature. I have tried to show that the chief requisite of a literature is a homogeneous language in which everything can be expressed that a people wishes to express. Scotland once had such a language, but we cannot return to it: to think so is to misunderstand history. That language still exists, in forms of varying debasement, in our numerous Scottish dialects; but these cannot utter the full mind of a people on all the levels of discourse. Consequently when we insist on using dialect for restricted literary purposes we are being true not to the idea of Scotland but to provincialism, which is one of the things that have helped to destroy Scotland. If we are to have a complete and homogeneous Scottish literature it is necessary that we should have a complete and homogeneous language. Two such languages exist in Scotland, and two only. The one is Gaelic and the other is English. There seems to me to be no choice except for these: no half-way house if Scotland is ever to reach its complete expression in literature. And of these two alternatives English is the only practicable one at present, whatever Gaelic may become in the future.

To say this is to say that Scotland can only create a national literature by writing in English. This may sound paradoxical: in support of it I can only advance my whole case in regard to the Scots language, as outlined in the first part of this book, and the contemporary case of Ireland. Irish nationality cannot be said to be any less intense than ours; but Ireland produced a national literature not by clinging to Irish dialect, but by adopting English and making it into a language fit for all its purposes. The poetry of Mr Yeats belongs to English literature, but no one would deny that it belongs to Irish literature pre-eminently and essentially. The difference between contemporary Irish and contemporary Scottish literature is that the first is central and homogeneous, and that the second is parochial and conglomerate; and this is because it does not possess an organ for the expression of a whole and unambiguous nationality. Scots dialect poetry represents Scotland in bits and patches, and in doing that it is no doubt a faithful enough image of the present divided state of Scotland. But while we cling to it we shall never be able to express the central reality of Scotland, as Mr Yeats has expressed the central reality of Ireland; though for such an end the sacrifice of dialect poetry would be cheap. The real issue in contemporary Scottish literature is between centrality and provincialism; dialect poetry is one of the chief supports of the second of these two forces; the first can hardly be said to exist at all. And until Scottish literature has an adequate language, it cannot exist. Scotland will remain a mere collection of districts.

As for the Scottish literary tradition, I have shown that it is lacking, but that at the same time it has more to give us than we realize. Miss Gray's anthology, *Scottish Poetry from Barbour to James VI*, should be on every bookshelf in Scotland, along with the poems of Burns. From it we can at least realize that Scottish literature was once a unity, and learn the elements of that unity. But Scottish literature by itself cannot provide a basis for a modern tradition, and it seems to me that nobody who has not absorbed the English literary tradition can even express the contemporary life of Scotland. We have, in any case, been deeply tinged with that tradition: so why not, like the Irish writers, take advantage of it?

There remains the social and political state of Scotland. That is different now from what it was in Scott's time, and the problem which faces us is therefore different. Scott saw Scottish manners inevitably melting into those of England, and he accepted the Union. Scottish manners have melted still more since he wrote, and now there is an increasing tendency to repudiate the Union. Scottish Nationalism has arisen mainly as a protest against this inevitable dissolution of manners. I do not believe in the programme of the Scottish Nationalists, for it goes against my reading of history, and seems to me a trivial response to a serious problem. I can only conceive a free and independent Scotland coming to birth as the result of a general economic change in society, after which there would be no reason for England to exert compulsion on Scotland, and both nations could live in peace side by side. But meanwhile it is of living importance to Scotland that it should maintain and be able to assert its identity; it cannot do so unless it feels itself a unity; and it cannot feel itself a unity on a plane which has a right to human respect unless it can create an autonomous literature. Otherwise it must remain in essence a barbarous country. That sense of unity can be preserved by an act of faith, as it was preserved in Ireland. Our task is to discover how this can be done; and I have tried to show how important the possession of a homogeneous language is for that end.

STIRLING DISTRICT LIBRARY